ADANMA

THE HEROIC GIRL

A STORY ABOUT THE SPIRIT OFTHE AFRICAN WOMAN

By Richards Ernest Chidi

ACKNOWLEDGEMENT

My thanks and gratitude be ascribed to God Almighty for the inspiration and grace to formulate this life-changing book for the younger generation.

The message therein is aimed at encouraging the younger ones to stand up for what is good and just and to take their destiny in their hands because life is not a bed of roses; but what one makes it to be.

Also,Iwant to use this platform to appreciate the following faith-based organizations thatare touching lives allover Africa through charity works for the poor.These include:

Late Prophet T. B Joshua, the founder of the Synagogue Church of all Nations, a man that lived all his life helping the poor, the disabled, widows and the elderlyseveral of whom are still mourning his early departure.May his soul rest in peace!I believe that his good works of charity will be counted for him by God as righteousness and He shall reward him with eternal life in His kingdom.

I also want to appreciate the T. Y. DANJUMA FOUNDATION for their great philanthropic works, scholarships and grants to the poor especially supporting the helpless girl children in her educational pursuit.May God bless T.Y DANJUMA FOUNDATION and all their associates!

I will not fail to appreciateeveryone who contributed to the success of the publicationof this book, these great people are:

- My wife Mrs Angela Chidi Richards and my children for supportingme both financially andprayerfully.
- My in-lawsMr and Mrs Collins Igbokwethe publisher andChief Editor of The Mail News.
- Mr and Mrs Henry Nwagu the MD/CEO of Obilizz Prints.
- Barrister S . O. Peters our legal adviser and solicitor

And to many other friends that encouragedme, I say thank you and God bless you all.

DEDICATION

It is my pleasure to dedicate this book to the honor of some great Nigerian women who have done well in their various fields and have exhibited excellence and other qualities of Africa such as hardwork and resilience.

i. Mrs. Stella ChinyeluOkoli the CEO of Emzor pharmaceutical company.

ii. DrNgoziOkonjoIweala one time Minister of Finance of Federal Repulblic of Nigeria and the first femaleDG of the World Trade Organization.

iii. MrsIbukunAwosika a one timechairman of First Bank of Nigeria, a successful business woman, author and motivational speaker who also the foundedtheFountain of Life Church Foundation.

iv. MrsFolorunshoAlakija who rose to become one of the richest african women inspite of her humble beginnings.

v. Dr. MrsObyEzekwesili an economic policy expert, former Minister of Education of Nigeria, humanitarian and advocate for transperency, accountability and good governance.

vi. OnyekaOnwenu a veteran singer, song writer, actress, human rights activist, jounalist and politician.

vii. MrsFunke AkindeleBello,aka Jenifaa Nigerian actress and film producer who has won the African Movie Academy Award for best actress.

viii. Genevieve Nnaji a very popular Nigerian actress, producer and a movie director that was the first to win the Africa Movie Academy Award for best actress.

ix. Linda Ifeomalkeji a famous Nigerian blogger, writer, online publisher and business woman who rose to fame by hardwork despite her very humble background .

x. Late Mrs. Dora Nkem Akunyili OFR an unforgettable woman of integrity who served as director for the Nigerian Food and Drug Administration and Control.

xi.Late Miss Tolulope Oluwatoyin Sarah Arotile the first ever woman combat helicopter pilot produced by Nigeria Air Force who contributed greatly to the combat operations against insecurity in the Northern States of Nigeria.

xii. Adaora Onyechere a famous journalist and television presenter who advocates for gender inclusiveness and equality in government.

TABLE OF CONTENTS

CHAPTER 1

A very long time ago, there lived a very hardworking old man.His name was Nze Nwaokoro and he had a lovely wife whose name he called (Obi Diya Alice) meaning the husband's heart.

Nze Nwaokoro hailed from Nsirimo Amaise of Umuahia South Local Government Area of Abia State. He had only one wife that gave birth to three children but they lost two to the cold hands of death during the Nigerian civil war. So, it was their only surviving good looking son named Nwokoma who grew up to care for his parents in their old age.

Nze Nwokoro was a professional hunter, a farmer and a palm wine tapper that was well known in the entire village because of his peaceful demeanour. He was a trouble-free man that neither took sides nor did he support evil. He was also a drummer for a masquerade group. Nze Nwokoro lived for 99 years before he died. His wife died 4 years later at the age of 85 but before their demise they both pronounced blessings upon their only surviving son.

Mazi Nwokoma grew up and took over his late father's occupation and also became popular within his village and other nearby villages and communities that relied on his ever fresh and sweet palm wine especially during their traditional ceremonies and annual festivals like the *New Yam Festival* and *Christmas.*

Whether during the farming season or dry season, people could always get palm wine to buy from him. Some even hired him to cultivate their lands during the farming season. It was during one of those seasons that he met his beautiful wife because beautiful women are noticed during dry season.

Nsirimo was a neighbouring town in the midst of many large towns. It shared river boundaries with Obizi town in Mbaise of Imo state. Nsirimo and Obizi villages had a lot in common. They had similar marriages, festivals and schools.

Also, because of their long cordial relationship, inter tribal marriages between both villages was commonplace.

On a certain day, Mazi Nwokoma was hired by the village head of Obizi Town who had heard about his lifestyle of hardwork and simplicity. His ability to entertain people by singing while working had also endeared him to many. In fact, his whereabouts was often determined whenever people heard someone singing masquerade songs with a loud voice at a distance while working with his hands. Many also enjoyed his charisma because he hardly got offended and he joked about almost everything.

CHAPTER 2

The Igbos in the southeasthern region of Nigeria are hardworking farmers who are also very good in commercial activities. They are also very accommodating especially to strangers and hired labourers. It is a tradition in Igbo land till date to hire labourers during the farming season and to take good care of them during and after the day's job by providing two meals for the labourers for lunch and dinner.

So, the village head and his beautiful wife prepared a delicious meal of African salad for Mazi Nwokoma their laborer and sent their first daughter Adaure to send the food and palm wine to him in the farm as his lunch.

Although it was a very hot afternoon, Adaure didn't complain but obediently went to the farm as she was instructed by her parents carrying with her a basket containing the delicious African salad and a keg of palm wine and a calabash of water.

As she approached from a distance, she began to hear the melodious loud voice of Mazi Nwokoma singing sweet masquerade songs that were inspiring him to carry out his farm work dilgently. By the time she got to the farm, she was amazed when she discovered that Mazi Nwokoma had cleared almost one and half plots of the two plots of land.

She greeted him in their local dialect saying, "Mazi, Ndewoo," meaning Well-done sir.

On hearing the sweet feminine voice, Mazi Nwokoma raised his head to see whose voice it was, behold behind him stooda pretty young fair in complexioned lady standing with a basket on her head, he responded with a smile "Eee Woo Ada Oma" Maning yes beautiful daughter, what have you come to do in this bush under this very hot afternoon he asked ?

And she replied my parents sent me to bring you this food for your lunch, it is an African Salad and Palm wine she said, MaziNwokoma responded, that's too kind of your parents, how did they know that African Salad use to be my favourite meal during hot afternoon like this, and by the way, why did you have to come under this hot sun? Pretty girls don't walk under the sun nor do they do hard works.

And she smiled and replied "Aaaa, I don't fear to work or go anywhere under the sun, because those that hide from the sun shall definitely have nothing to eat during the raining season.

Who taught you that? My parent didof course, she responded."EziOkwuNwaoma" Meaning "that's true talk" then

MaziNwokoma walked down to her as he droppedhis bush clearing staff and his cutlasses , first he lifted the basket off her head, dropped it to the ground and drank the cool stream water from the calabash before sitting down to enjoy the African salad and the palm wine.

Aduare said to him, "Mazi, you are a very hard working person just as my father said you are, and I have seen it. It's just noon and you are almost through with this farm. my father will be very happy with you, that's true my dear, I don't joke with my work, because time waits for no one, people knows me for that.

While you eat sir, let me walk around the farm to gather firewood's and pluck some bush pears for my mother, OdinmaNwaOma"Meaning is okay, beautiful girl said MaziNwokoma" but be very careful and watchful over sharp objects and harmful insects please let nothing hurt you, yes sir thank you she said and walked away.

Before she could come back, MaziNwokoma has emptied the plate of African Salad, leaving no crumb and he began to sip his palm wine alsohavinghis snuff box on his left hand anda second dose of it in his right fingerthumb, having snuffedthe first dose.

CHAPTER 3

Adaure asked him,Mazi, did you enjoy the food?Yes very much, African salad is always my favorite dish anytime especially during a time like this, how I wish mypotential wife will be able to be preparing such for me like this anytime I needs it?

Adaure replied, "What do you mean sir: are you not married? Yes, I am not married yet, why and what are you waiting for? She asked, I amwaiting on God to give me a woman that will love me and accept me as I am, because I am not educatedand I am not iving in the city like other young men.

I am surprise at hearing this from you sir, how do you eat and who cooks for you sir? No one my dear, I can cook all types of foods by myself and what about you Adaoma? I know you are not married yet, but if will, can you marry a man like me?

She laughed hahahaha and asked him what kind of question is this you are asking me? Adaure is a very pretty girl with an open teeth,Mazi Nwokoma saw her set of teeths and fell in love with her the more seeing her beautiful white open teeth.

And she said, not at al, I am not thinking of marriage now, I am still a young virgin girl, besides I am still in school.

There and then Mazi Nwokoma began to toasther with praises, saying to her "you are such a beautiful daughter with a very good character; I have never seen a girl like you before, behold your open teeth, your long hairs, shining skin and pointed nose.

She laughed and replied, please sir stop it I am just a little girl of 18yearsthat knows no man, I don't have such in my mind for now, besides my parents will kill me if I try anayrubish act.

MaziNwokoma hearing that she never knew a man at 18 years, hebecame more interested and then proposed to her, "Adamaranma, can you allow me to Marry you? I have been praying to meet a good reserved girl like you and today I have found you, please allow me to marry you I beg you to accept my proposal,I have enough lands to farm and I will treat you as my queen, like you know I am a very good hunter,every day my trap will always catch bush meats for us to eat like that rabbit over there that I killed today in this farm which you will take home to your father as you go from here

No you need not always eat every meat your trap caught, sometimes you shall sell them to save money, if I will marry any man, I will make sure such a man saves money, hearing all the wise talks from her mouth, MaziNwokomawas pleased and persuaded hermore withsweet toasting languages thatshe melted and began to fall in love with him and she said, if you promise to take good care of me, then I will say Yes".

MaziNwokoma became very happy and promised her, heaven on earth, and then she said, you have to tell my parents first and Mazi promised to do so as quickly as possible.

CHAPTER 4

That evening, the village head had prepared thebush meat which MaziNwokoma killed from the farm, he also provided enough fresh Palm wine, while his wife the mother of Adaurehad prepared enough delicious food waiting for their guest.

MaziNwokoma went there that night in company with his best friend at whose house he choose to lodge, because he could not return back to his village that night,already he has told hisfriend about his new found young girl to marry, his friend was interested to meet the pretty girl as she was described and to know the family she came from.

 As they arrived, they met the village head seated already outside with his friend Mr. Ikenga , they were there with a jar of palm wine and some roasted pieces of the bush meats they were eating with fresh pepper sauce, while waiting for MaziNwokomaarrival.

The village head welcomed him together with his friend thathe came with, the village head introducedMaziNwokoma to his ownfriendand they offered them seats and brought out more drinks and they began todrink as they discuss about the days job experience.

After a few minutes of the guest arrival, Adaure and her mother came out to set the table for the dinner and the food was served,Adaure hearing the voice of her proposed suitor , she was happy within herself also she was so afraid of her parents, not knowing what theirreactions would be,in caseif MaziNwokomachoosed to makehis intentions known to them thatnight.

After they have eaten the deliciousAcharaand Egusi Soup, that was cooked with enough meats, dry fish and snails, the village head brought out the well prepared bush meat garnishedwith fresh pepper and more Palm wine, they continued to eat and drInk, discussing the events of the farm and other relative issues affecting the community including high cost of commodities in the market and insecurity,there and then, MaziNwokoma opened up to his host his intension to ask the hand of the villag had daughter in Marriage.

CHAPTER 5

MaziNwokoma demanded for the attention of the village head for a discussion, as he said, chief please permit me to place a demand on you this night, and the chief responded, okay MaziNwokoma speak my two ears are widely opened, said the village head, he started by giving the villages head praises for his hospitality and generosity, after showering him with praises, before placing his demand.

And the village head responded, Mazi what is it? I don't understand the meaning of all these praises you are pouring on me this night, I hope you are not trying to ask me about money? Because I have no money to lend out to anybody this farming season, let me tell you before you continue.

MaziNwokoma replied and said, no sir, it is not about money but something more important than that is in my mind to ask from you, and what is it that is more important to a young man like you than money?Okay, I wish to hear what it is about?

MaziNwokoma began first by clearing his throat with coughing and he stammered and said, emmmm, emmmm, I saw a riped orange at your back yardtoday that attracted my eyes, which I want to beg for your approval to allow me to pluck it.

The village head understood the parable quite clear, but pretended not understanding theproverbhe was given, he said to him, Idon't understand your parables, what do you mean by riped orange at my backyard? Come out open or are you seeing double?

MaziNwokoma looked at his friend eye to eye, his friend smiled at him as he winked his eyes on him, given him moral and boldness to speak up,MaziNwokoma sat upright and faced the village head as he greeted him again, he started his stories again by reminding the village head about the cordial relationship between his village and that of the ObiziMbaise people, also he said that it is his desire that the woman he willmarry shall come from this part of the village.

Therefore, it seem to me that I have found my missing ribs here in your family among your beautiful and well trained daughters, that is the meaning of my parable of the riped orange at your backyard, I am asking the hand of your first daughter in marriage , I plead toyou to allow me marry your elderly daughter/Adaure.

"The village head burst into laughter hahahahaha, and called on him MaziNwokoma,, is it what you are beating around the bushto say since, why stammering to speak and why biting your tongue ?My friend I know you are tipsy that is why you are talking and stammering, matters like this are not good to be discouss when drunked because I can see that you are drunk.

Not at all I am not drunk, I am with my right sense of mind, I will like to have you as myfather in-law please sir accept me, any way,It is not a bad request you have made but tell me, when and where did you meet my daughter Adaure? And who toldyo that my daughter is up to the age of marriage? Besides you should know that shoes has sizes, do you think you are fit and wealthy enough to ask the hand of a royal daughter of mine in marreiage?

Is it not just today you saw her at the farm, how come you have fixed your eye on her for marriage? Or have you met her anywhere before? By the way,is she aware of this you are telling me this night?

MaziNwokomasaid yes she is , we just met today as she brought me food and we have discussed and she accepted my proposal, the village head shouted oh my forefathers, and he asked MaziNwokoma, are you sure of this you are telling me?Andare you sure you did not touch my draughter right there in the bush?If you did, I will kill you this night, I think you are talking from the influence of alcohol not with your clear eyes, you are drunked by this sweet fresh Palm wine.

Aaaaa not at all my chief, I am not drunk sir,he responded and I didn't torch her, may the gods of our land strike me dead if I did, hearing that the village head cooled his anger and said "okay if that be the case, I should take you serious, however as for me I know your late father and your mother, I know many families in your village who are my friends, therefore you will have my support if it is the will of God for you and my daughter to get married, but you still have to give her some time to reach the age of marriage, she is just 18 years, what does she know about marriage at this her tender age?.

Anyway, I think I should let my wife hear theseyour tales by moonlight, you just told me, this your request is bigger than what one ear should hear,excuse me he said, as he called on his wife,Obidiyaa, Obidiyaa, please come I need you here and she responded quickly from her kitchen thinking that they needed more food.

As she rushed out from her kitchen, she askedNnaanyiwhat's the matter?Do our visitors need more food?Not at all the husband responded, and then what's the matter? Why the urgent call? My heart flew away when I heard the call, Sit down my wife and listen for yourself what MaziNwokoma is asking from us, that is why I called you as I can't tell if he is drunk.

What is it Nnanyi, tell me my ears are open to hear, the village headsaid,MaziNwokoma after the food, he began a story I could not understand, he said he wants to marry our daughter, he said he and our daughter have agreed to marry each other, therefore he is seeking our consent and approval to their marriage agreement, look at him before us let him repeat himself to you for your hearing.

Eeeewooo!!!! Is that true? As she lifted her two hands to her head saying, wonders shallnevr end, when did that began?MaziNwokoma, where did you meet my daughter, she asked him?How long have you known her? So this little girl is spoilt already?

Youmean you did not see girls of your class in your villageNsirimoto marry?, why my dauhter? She turned to her husband and asked, Nnaanyi, what did you tell him on this matter? Or is it your arrangement with him to give away our daughter to any how man? Is this the reason why you hired him to work for us, on a secrete arrangement with him to marry our daughter?

The vllage head ranted enough,how can you ask me such nasty questions? Why should I make secrete arrangement to give away our daughter to a man whose family name is not known anywhere even in his own community, while I have sons of my big men friends and sons of my fellow chiefs that are begging to marry our daughter?

Is it not your daughter who decided toridicule our family reputation, trying to drag my reputation to the mod by accepting the marriage proposals from a poor farmer?, the whole thing came to me by surprise and unexpected also, as such I have not given him my whole consent, because I am tempted to also think that as a mother you are, you knew about thisarrangement before me,because you are more closer to our daughter than I do, you should know more of her secrete and feelings than me, don't you?the husband asked.

The wife hearing the response of her husband, flared up and said, my husband how dare you think I should know everything about these children? How could I know when they are very secretive even to their mothers?

Anyway as for me, my daughter is still a little girl, my wish for her is to continue with her education as to get a good work and a rich husband when her time comes, so that when my daughter givesbirth, I will go for Omugbwo in the city, therefore these arrangement, will not get my support at all count me out of it.

However, it is not a bad request you have made she said, we knew your Family both your late father and mother also we knew you to be a very nice hard working young man that can make a good family, but that will not be the reason for me to allow you marry my daughter.

Nnaanyi that is my own response and opinion to this matter, because I want the best for my daughter,a man that will take good care of her and both shall live in the city, that's what I want,not the man that will turn her tobecome a village womantomorrow like the way they tuned me to in this village.

 Obi diyaa, will youshut up your moth there, what are you trying to tell the world?Are You trying to say that I turned you to a village woman? Looking at you and other women in the city, who looks more healthy and attractive? Are you lacking anything in this village? At this time the village head friend added his voice to the argument by supporting the opinion of his friends wife, he said, Lolo you have a very good point, times have changed, the yesterday system of marriage ,cannot work in this present time, women are no longer made to be left uneducated this time like the women of old, therefore to end this argument, we still needs to hear from the girl in question, but as for me, I will advise you give the little girl a chance to get good education before getting married, the young man can wait for her if he so desires.

Mean while,MaziNwokoma becamefrightened by their argument because he had already falling deeply in love with Adaure. Therefore he began to plead and promised to be a better son in-law to the family, saying you know I am an orphan the only surviving child of my late parents, I want to be part of your family, please take me as your son in-law I am begging.

 Well, we need to hear from our daughter first the father said, just as my friend do suggested, we shall not be the one to choose suitor for her, and we shall not kick against the will of God, neither should we stop her from making her choice of man,but I do not think thatyou must be the one, but let's call her and hear from her.

CHAPTER 6

Adaure, Adaure, Adannayaaa, " Mamaaa" she responded and she came forth from the backyard, walking up slowly, the Father asked her fiercely, did you reach any agreement of marriage with MaziNwokoma? She did not say a word because she was afraid of her father'won't you speak? Did you have any agreement of marriage with MaziNwokoma and where and when did you meet each other?

How long have you known him? She looked at her mother's face, she shouted at her and said, stop looking at me and answer your father before I descend on you right now, her mother's face was looking so furious and full of anger, she looked at MaziNwokoma,he was almost down to his knees sweating on his face at that cool hourof the night because of the heat of interrogations.

Therefore, Adauresummoned courage to answered her father, Yes Papa she replied, it was today we met at the farm as I went to send him food at the farm, there he saw me and promised to marry me, then what did you tell him as your response to his request?, Papa I told him no that I am still a little girl, then he continued to request for my acceptance and promised me good future, then I told him yes, if he can take good care of mejustthe way my father cares for my mother, and he promisedme, then I told him to seek my father and mother consent first, whatever they said, will determine what shall be done.

The father looked at her closely and asked her, did you do anything with him? I mean did he tuch you right there in the bush? , no papa he did nothing to me, do you mean you accepted to get married to a man at 18 years?, don't you want to go to school anymore?

Yes Papa I have loved him, allow me to marry him, the mother flared up and told her to shut up her mouth, how come you saw a man only one day, you succumbed to his lies, are you that cheap? Don't youknow that men are cheats and liars? How much do you know about this man that you are crazy for?

Adaure was speechless and sober almost crying, saying she wants to marry him, the father was very mad at her, but at a second thought he decided to respect the wish of her daughter because he loved her so dearly that he could not withstand watching her cry.

 He said, my daughters go back to your room, your wish has settles the case, Young man letdrink and go home to sleep overyour request, you will get our reply in due time.

Meanwhile, go home and rethink, perhaps you are drunk and doesnot mean all you have told us, goand come back again to received our final answer.

After the departure of the visitors, the village head and his wife sat their daughter down and the mother began to ask her why does she think it is proper for her to dabble into marriage at this tender age?, do you know that marriage is saddled with lots of responsibilities and ups and downs? It is beyond living together with a man maybe you don't know, are you with your eyes? Yes Mama she responded.

And the father said to her, my daughter in case you don't know, no woman from our family who has gone to husband house, ever returns backhome after except on a visit, because such will not be welcomed from you, do not say you were not told therefore think twice, look well before you leap, as for me, I will not stop you from getting married to him if you so wish, I will send our message of acceptance to him as soon as possible, this conclusions did not go down well with the mother.

A week after, the village head send word across to MaziNwokoma, asking him to come, onreceiving the invitation MaziNwokoma was unsure of what the outcome of the invitation would be.

But to his amazement, his request was considered and accepted, and he was very pleased that he thanked the Village Head and his beautiful wifefor granting him his request and he promised to love and care for Adaure till death do them part.

Adaure became very happy inside of her she said, papa thank you for been there for me, and she thanked her mother too, while her mother walked back to her kitchen not very happy because her husband has ruled over the mater.

CHAPTER 7

MaziNwokoma with joy, notified his family members of his intention to get married soon, it was an unbelievable story to many thatheard about it,due to the fact that everyone knew him to be a man that jokes at all times, people hardly take his words serious when it comes to issues of getting married.

So he went on describing the family where which he found his wife, many that knew the family, were surprised and they praised him saying he is highlyfavored to find a wife from such a royal family.

Quickly, arrangement was made for him to pick the traditional bride list;ituses to be celebrated as it is the first step to every traditional marriage preparation, known to be Introduction or engagement stage.

On that day, he went with selected family elders and with few of his friends, they were all well dressed and caring a jar of palm wine and a bottle of seaman dry gin, as they reached there, they met a set of elders both men and women and youths and children, they were wellreceived by the family, cola nut was presented to them by the eldest man from the bride to be family, after which they were asked to officially explain the reason for their visit.

Following the tradition, the eldest man from MaziNwokoma family, stood up onbehalf of the groom family to offered his greetings to the village head and to the entire family, thanking them for receiving them as august visitors, he started his talk with a proverb that said,when a chicken is seen running in the broad day afternoon, is either it is pursuing something or something is pursuing it, and the people said it is true.

He said, this our visit to your family todayis not a bad visit, we are here to extend a hand shake of friendly relationship with yourfamily that will last from generation to generations, that is the purpose of our visit to your family.

Oh, you are welcome, your visit is good, but we are yet to understand in full what you are trying to say, please make it plain for everybody to understand, what kind of hand shake?

Okay my fellow elder, you know that proverbs is like the red palm oil for which we use in eating roasted yam, yes what I am trying to explain is that, this Our sonMaziNwokoma, whomeverybody knows very well , as a hard working person across our community, came home one day from his work, and told us that he saw a very beautiful ripped orange in your family that caught his mind, as such we came to seek your permission to allow us plug that beautiful orange for our son.

to cut my long talk short, we have come to ask the hand of your first daughter in marriage for our son MaziNwokoma, that is our mission, and here is our drink for which we came to introduce our selves and to knock at your door.

The eldest man from the village head, again stood up to welcome the visitors for the second time, he said now you have spoken, you are welcome, your visit is a good and honorable oneand we are glad to receive you people to our family, and we have seen the drink you brought to knock at our door.

 Butbefore we could proceed further to drink, we need to confirm if our daughter is aware of this visit and the purpose, we must call her out to show us who among these able young men here, is asking her hands in marriage, and both family agreed in one voice to the sayings.

The father whispered to the mother, there and then the women went inside her mother's room to usher the young girl in and she was asked by eldest man, do you know why everybody gathered in your family today? She answered, yes sir I know, it's because of me she said, do you know any man called MaziNwokoma ?Yes I know him, do you accept to marry him? Yes I accepted his marriage proposal, and I did promise to marry him.

Do you mean we should receive the drink from them and drink? Yes Papa receives and drink she said, can you show us which personamong these young men that asked your hand in marriage? She stood up shyly and moved straight to the real manMaziNwokoma and everybody began to clap their hands.

The eldest man from the bride family stood up again to bless the drinks and cola with prayer after which, every one began to feast as both families have agreed and accepted the marriage introduction, also the marriage bride list was given to him at the cost of N2,000 00 (Two thousand naira)for each list, which he paid.

CHAPTER 8

As they were eating and drinking, the eldest man from the bride family stood up to inform them abouttheirfamily bridefour (4) pages that contain all requirements for the traditional marriage.

He told them to meet with their family secretary and treasurer to pick up the list at the cost of Two Thousand Naira Only for each list,(N2000 X 4), he also told them to go back home for their preparation for the traditional marriage .

The groom family pleaded for a discount of one thousand naira on each page of list, which they were granted .

THE FOUR LISTS WERE:

1. THE MOTHERS LIST.

2.THE FATHERS LIST.

3. THE FAMILY LIST.

4.THE YOUTHS LIST.

The family received the lists, glanced at the content, the items were numerous and all the required items were written in doubles as traditional marriagedemands according to tradition, it is afixed family list, kept from generation to generations.

To some families it might be lesser or higher but the beauty is that, on the very dayof the occasion, when both family meet in the inner room for dowry payment, the contents will raise a debates and negotiationby both families and most times many of the listeditems, willbewaved away andoverlooked by bride parents for the In Law relationship sake.

MaziNwokoma received all thelists from his would be inlaws in good faith, reaching back home, he began the preparation as he fixed the date for the traditional marriage,having notifiedall his family members and friends about the list and the fixed date.

The entire family members began their individual preparation, their youth's cultural group which he belongs as an active member; also began to practice new songs.

As the fixed day was approaching, preparation were going onheavily, friends and relations were invited, Adaure also began her own preparations, more especially, her traditional beauty make ups was her concern, she chooses her hair styling to be plated with black wool trade and long standing style, she also made arrangement for traditional tattoo skin designerandher bridal cloths weremade of bids as a princes.

CHAPTER 9

What a beautiful day it was for Adaure and Maxi Nwokoma as both families prepared very well for the occasion, many people followedMaziNwokomabecause they loved him ,both families invited their friends, more especially the village head invited many of his friends to witness the occasion of his first daughters marriage, the occasion was very colorful, there was traditional dancers and cultural singers, the elders of the both families began the traditional marriage process, the bride family members sat one side while the groom family seated opposite side and the bride familysecretary stood up with the original marriage list, calling out the listed items line by lines, while the both families began the arguments and the bargains on the items.

It was like an open market bargaining, as most of the items were debated upon with strong harsh voice of negotiations disagreements among the two families, as if they were going to disagreeintoto, but on every list, they came to mutual agreements until the whole list were treated and completed with peace and joy.

what an interesting culture it is, butat the end of it all, it was like no money was spent, because the father and the mother of the bride stood up and said," we are not selling our daughter, the only amount we need for our daughters dowry is(N50) Fifty Naira only. This remains the beautiful aspects of Igbo marriage culture, the cheapest allover Nigeria, but people from other tribes and regions do not know about this beautiful culture ofIgbopeople.

After the bride price was received and settled, then the celebration began properly, the cultural singers began to play one of MaziNwokoma best song and people began to dance in jubilation, food and drinks were surplus enough to satisfy every guest.

At that time Adaure was made to be inside away from the crowed, while her husband was sitting in a much hidden Corner waiting for his wife to fish him out with a cup of palm wine.

The master of the ceremony (MC) a comedian that is well known by his stage name as ,(MC. RAMPIOUS)known to be the best that could hold any crowd with jokes and riddles, he is also a singer, he announced that it was time for Adaure the beautiful bride of MaziNwokoma to come out with a dance for people to see and celebrate with her and for her to search out for her husband among the youths in the crowed, he also told the crowd to get ready to dance with the celebrants

At this special awaited time, she demanded for a special popular traditional marriage song from MrFlavor, the best African high life singer, titled (ADA, ADA) as the traditional singers were playing thebeautiful tone for her,she began to come out with a very beautiful dancing steps, followed by many spinsters who are yet to marry, beautiful young girls, friends and her family members, the song was her choice song and everybody both young and old loves the song and they all stood up to danced to the music, as she was coming out, every eye were on her, people began to clap while some stood to spray money on her including her father, mother and friends'

As the celebration was on, she went before her father, knelt down before him to receive a cup of palm wine, she took thecup and danced round the crowd searching for her husband, she danced round from one table to the other, been accosted by other men, some jokingly said to her, I am the right one give me the cup, others said I am he, let me have the drink.

yet she refused to give the cup of wine to the wrong man ,she kept dancing and searching for her real man, till she finally find him where he was hiding behind group of friends, as she danced to him, reaching where he was , she knelt before him and gave him the cup of wine, which he gladly received from her, people applauded as he received the cup of wine from her joyfully, he drank the wine and took her by his right hand, lifted her up and they began to dance , dance till they danced back to the bride father, knelt before him as he received the empty cup from them, showered his blessing on them as they continuedwith the celebration till the end of the occasion.

After the occasion, the newly married couples received their parental blessing and went home together that night with other spinsters that accompanied Adaure to her husband house according to culture.

CHAPTER 10

MaziNwokoma began to live with his newly married wife, never wanted her to do any hard work nor to mixed up with people, he was thinking of her beauty and was so afraid of other young men advancing to his new wife.

Adaure became tired of staying indoors doing no work, most time MaziNwokoma would cook for her also followed her to the stream to fetched water together.

One day,he met his wife sitted at the corner of their bed in sober mood which he hates seeing, when he noticed her sad mood, he was so troubled that he asked her,my dear what's the matter? Why are you in this mood while I am here with you? She didn't want to speak until the husband called her different lovely pet names he also gave her money to buy whatever she needed.

Then she smiled and told him that she needed to start doing something like other women, because she was tired of staying idle since she got married to him, she said it is not wise for a woman to remain a full time house wife this present time, leaving the family responsibility to the husband alone that is not a wise decision, I am tired of staying idle ineed to create my own means of daily income, I won't continue to stay at home lik this she said, her husband saw reasons why she should be allowed to work as to help te family, yet he insisted that she should remain at home for him.

So the husband responded to her, I didn't marry you for you to do anything; I married you for you to enjoy my money and to give me beautiful children,why trouble yourself? Go and give me food to eat also bring me that overnight left over palm wine let me start drinking before the food is ready, but she insisted and said to him, if you refused me to work, I will return back to my parents,

 That would be the last thing MaziNwokoma would allowed to happen, hearing that from his wife, hequickly changed his sitting position and he called upon her to explain his reasons why he wanted her to remain indoor.

He said, my fear for not allowing you do anything has been because ofthese young men around in our village, you know you are very beautiful, I don't want any man to take you from me, the wife burst into laughter hahahahahaha, is that the reason why you refused me working? No wonder you kept policing me even when I am going to stream?

Please my husband remembers you married me a virgin, was there no young men in my community that I should have messed up with before I got married to you? Such can never happen fear not, I have enough good moral up bringing from my parents, besides I know that it is a sin to commit adultery or fornication,therefore I am for you and for you alone. MaziNwokoma, hearing that, he smiled and called her NWANYI NKEM OMA, meaning my own beautiful wife.

They came to agreed terms; the agreement was for her to begin a petty trading ofcrayfish at the village Marketsquare and never to do hard works because it seems she was already pregnant at that time.

CHAPTER 11

MaziNwokoma was blessed with very beautiful children,their firstchild was a girl whom they named (Adanma,) a very beautiful girl,few years later, God multiplied the familywith three more children,whose names were,(Chibuzor), the only male child,(Ngozi) the second daughter and(Chioma)theirlast daughter.

MaziNwokoma, been a farmer,a hunter and a professional Palm wine tapper, had little or no educational agendas for the girl children, all his conciren was to teach them farming and for girl children to get married quick.

Everyday, he goes out very early in the morning after using hot drink tosay his prayers, he always callupon ChukwuAbiama , the(God of Abraham,) also he calls upon his ancestorsasking for their daily protection and blessings.

 After that, he puts on his hunting and farming hat, picked up his calabash, hung it on his old bicycle with his very sharp cutlasses, he saddled down the forest while his black hunting dog continuing running after him behind as he rode down through the bush tracks to the forest to check his traps and to tap his wine.

Most times his trap will catch some bush meats for him,whom he brings home to sell to villagers, and most times he gave some to his wife for the family to eat.

Everyone knows his wife in the village market, as she sells crayfish, vegetables, red oil, salt and other food items to support his husband in providingfor the family.

Their children were alwaysat home doing domestic works like, breaking of palm kennelsseeds and other works, even during school sections andholidays , Adanma was very on happily, because they needed to join their mates at school.

MaziNwokoma and his wife priority was to train the girl children to become good farmers and good house wives to whomever that will marry them, as he uses his beautiful wife as a good example for a good and hardworking woman the girl children should emulate.

One market day,MaziNwokoma and his wife harvested baskets of cassava,Vegetables, together with gallons of red oil and palm cannels, all these they took to market for sale, whileAdanma and her siblings weresent toweed grasses in their mother's cassava farm, as they were going,Adanma was very unhappy as she grumbled all through yet doing the work.

But as time went by, Adanma continue to disturb their parents on the need to go to school, One day their fatherdecided to take themto the community Primary School for enrolment and Adanma was tested by the head teacher and she was found to be verybrilliant girl that can cope at the Upper Primarybecause, she was close to 10year and too old to be in lower class with the youngerkid.

Then it was a closer period to the common entrance and promotional examination, so the head mistress decided fixing her at primary 5, but the fear and doubt of everyone was how she could cope, but she was very confident of herself to pass the exams if she studies hard, because she was very determined to join her age mates that were already in different Secondary Schools ahead of her, she knew she was far behind,but she never minded nor did she felt ashamed of been in the primary school together with kids far below her age , rather she was very glad to have started schooling.

In the school, children plays togetherin groups of friends and classmates, playing different games among eachother,Adanma was new at school and did not havemuch friends than Mary her classmate,Adanma was the shy type,coupled to the fact that she was not having good school uniform like other girls, so she always feels inferior most times before pupils, also her classmates who knew her father very well, nick named her(Adanma thehunters daughter), this gave herlots of concern and worries her emotionally.

Amazingly during break period, she would be found busy copying past noteswhich she borrowed from her classmate Marythe only person she could refer as her friend, While other pupils were out in the field playing football, cards and other games, but not so with her,most times, she is found seating underthe mango tree with her only friend reading and discussing about their future ambitions, and Mary was trilling herwith the stories about life in the city of Lagos where her parents resides.

The stories about Lagoswas very fascinating to Adanmas hearing, that she continues to imagine how beautiful the city of Lagos would be,and she asked Mary, will you be going to Lagos during the next holiday?Yes I will, but it must be after the common entrance examinations Mary replied.

CHAPTER 12

Mary, will you please tell your parents about me so that I might join you to Lagos to spend the holidaysshe asked? Mary laughed hahahaha, do you mean you will love to follow me to Lagos? Yes I wish to, that will be nice Mary said, I promised I must tell my parents about you coming to Lagos with me to spend the holidays this time, but you need some money for transportation, yes I know I should and I have some savings I could use for that, in my savings I have up to five thousand naira (5000.00) savings, Mary laughed at her, do you think that going toLagos s is a journey to the next village one can ride to on a bicycle? You need up to ten thousand naira even more to go to Lagos.

Really, is it that expensive?hahahahah Mary laughed, and said that's the amount required, anyway that's not a big problem I will save more money before then Adanma said.

Mary asked, how will you get such money to save? Will you steal from your parents? Or do you have a guy dating you secretly? God forbidme to try such rubbishAdanma replied, most time I help people to weed their farms after the job, I get paid also my parents do gave me some money my pocket money and up keep as a growing girl, all these I will save to travel with you to Lagos.

Mary was sober hearing her story and she said, Just try and save more money before then, when we gets to Lagos, myparents will take us to places for sightseeing and they will buy us many good things and you shall meet my Lagos friends both boys and girls,Adanma became very happy with her friend Mary and she begged her never to change mind on her promise.

May laughed and said I promise never to change mind but do you think that your parents will allow you go to Lagos? Yes they have to as soon as I get home I shall tell my mum first and she will let my father know about it,Adanma said.

Mary asked, what if your fathers say no to your going to Lagos with me when your mother tells him, what will you do Mary asked? My father gives my mother what so ever she ask from him, he can hardly say no to my mother's request each time,Adanma responded .

From that moment they became more tight friends been very fond of each other as noticed by everyone at school including teachers, Most times, Mary will spends her money for Adanma during free periods and also she gives her some of her nice dresses; because she realized that her friend does not have much, but unfortunately to Mary, Adanma does not fancy collecting things from people, sheused to be very contented with the little her parent could provide for her, while Mary likes seeing her dressing fine with the dresses she gives her.

Reaching home, Adanma was very excited that she told her mother of her plans to join her friend Mary to visit Lagos during the next holidays for the first time, have you told your father about this the mother asked? I have not because I don't know howto present it to papa, maybe you will help me to discuss that with him in your private time with him, and I would need ten thousand naira (10,000) for the journey.

Now it was time for common entrance examinations,Adanma joined her mother in the kitchen where she was preparing night dinner for the family and she told her about her dream to continue with schooling if she could pass the common entrance examinations and her ambition was to become a medical doctor when she grows up.

Her mother who knew the strength and the financial background of the family called on her, "Adanma,Adanma' she replied "Mama "the mother said to her, sit down my daughter, let us put head's togetherto talk about this your schooling ambition, which you were talking about, I know it is good for people to be educated where there is money in the family, but can you please think about something else that would be easier than this your schooling, schooling, you are singing about.

Hearing the mother's suggestions, she flared up and said, Mama I don't want to hear that from you and Papaplease, and I don't have any other plans than to go to school.Take it easy and listen to me my daughter "Don't you think it will be better for you to forget about this schooling idea and think of something very easy to learn, Such as hair dressing occupation or Tailoringso you can get married quick as to help me and your father, do you want us to die? We don't havemoney for your schooling ambition that is what I am trying to let you understand.

 You know you are a very pretty girl, also remember that girls are like flowers that shines today and fades away tomorrow, you know how poor your parents are, we cannot afford to pay the bill of sending you to Secondary School, should in case you pass this common entrance extermination, I will advise you to stop it thereand think about something else or get married now to a man that will help our family.

'Adanma became speechless and the mother said, my daughter I am talking to you, reason with us and say something, what do you think concerning all I have been saying since.?

Adanma began to cry and continue to cry before her mother, while her mother continues to speak, saying my daughter stop crying, I am telling you the true situation of our family,which you have known already before now that we don't have money for your schooling and no one to run to.

Adanma said, Mama there is nothing you will tell me that will make me change my mind or drop my dream of going to school, Papa has lands he should sale oneor two of his properties and send us to school, that is how other families are doing to train their children no one has it all.

The mother responded, that's true my dear for families that has enough lands to sale, how many lands do we have? Your father must not hear these from you, he will be mad at you because you want to spoil his plans as he is looking forward to be the best yam farmer in the village as to receive the yam farmers title of EZE JI,(king of yam farmers).

Mama of what importance is the EZE JI Title to papa, compare to his daughter education? That is selfishness if Papa could thinks that way Adanma said. And the mother responded shot up your mouth, I think I know why youare crying, you just want to join your mates at Secondary School that is all, but have you forgotten that most of them there, have theirparentslives at the city doing white man jobs and business? But we are here doing farm work, so my daughter listen to me and follow your mother good advice, your future and destiny is in God's hand even those that didn't attend any form of schooling still survives through other vocations, therefore if you did not get education, you can still get good handwork and marry a good husband that will take good care of you, please do it quick so I cansee mygrand children now that I am still a young woman to help you care for them.

Adanma responded to her Mother "Mama you are not wishing me well by all these you are saying, my teacher told us that education is the best legacy every parent must give to their children, because it is the key to success and it guarantees good life and riches, I want to go to school so as to help the family.

And the mother rose up and shouted her down loudly,saying keep quiet, can you notunderstand? What do you mean that I your mother that gave birth to you after my (9 months of pregnancy pains) that I am not wishing you well? Do you want your father to steal, who will pay your school fees if you pass this common entrance examination?

 Those your teachers who are talking what they don't know, how rich are they? Don't you know that only the children of the rich gets good jobs after schooling? Not so with the children of the poor, besides you are a girl our people does not value girls child education, your concern at this your beautiful age now,should be to get married and settle down with a nice man, my daughter forget about the schooling agenda, we cannot carry the load of sponsoring you to the   collage if you pass?.

Adanma responded with a loud crying voice, Mama God will pay my school fees, I will go to school like other girls, I have an ambition that I must pursue, as she continue crying and the Mother said "God will come down from Heaven to pay the school fees, is it not this your fathers Palm wine and his farming jobs that we are living on? Hasyour father any helper that he should run to for your sake?

Adanma replied "God will help me, as she continued crying and her mother also continued to shout her down, MaziNwokoma came out from his resting place, having in his hand his long woolen towel which he uses to drive away and to kill sun flies and mosquitoes when relaxing on his easy chair outside.

He called on his wifetwice" Obidiaaa, Obidiaaaa" what's the matter? , what's happening in my family? Why is Adannayaa my daughtercrying?What's the matter did anybody die? Somebody talk to me.

His wife responded, is it not your daughter and her schooling ambition, simple because I told her that we cannot afford to carry the load of her going to college that was why she wants to kill herself.

MaziNwokoma asked, is that all? then he turned to her daughter, and said my daughter stop crying and listen to your mother advice, " I am surprise that you my daughter do not want to reason along with your mother and pity us your parents, what you are demanding is very good but try to understand that your parents are very poor, besides you are a girl child what do you need schooling for?Just dry your tears, after your common entrance examination, Ipray you get married quickly to any man, like your mother my lovely wife did, she was 18years when I married her.

Adanma stood up and said to her father, God forbid that I should get married without getting goodeducation; my teacher told us that only through education one can get rich, it is after my schooling that I will think of getting married.

Papa it is because you and Mama did not go to school, that is why you cannot understand the importance of education and that is more reason why our family is the poorest in this village.

The father shouted at her,taaaaaaaaah, shut up that your dirty mouth, what does your teachers know about life, are all your teachers rich people?Don't we see and know those of them that buyfood on credits from people most times in this village, are they rich people yet they feeds on credit? Will you stop telling us that nonsense stories ,Adanma walked to her room remained there crying while her siblings where consoling her.

CHAPTER 13

It was few weeks to the Common Entrance Examination, one day the school headmaster gathered all the students at the assembling ground to address them and to prepare their mind towards the soon and fast approaching Common Entrance Examination.

The headmaster said to them "Common Entrance Exams, are a very important external examination that is higher than ordinary class room examination, it is an examination that will determine those of you that will proceed to the secondary school next year, he warned the entire student that any one that did not spend extra time on reading, he or she might not pass the exam and any student caught cheating during the exams will be arrested by the police and dearly punished, therefore I urge all of you to put in your best and do our school proud.

Those that will pass with very good and highest grade might be lucky to get scholarship from the state government or from traditional rulers or from any rich person in your community.

Hearing this,Adanma began to pray in her heart and said to herself "I will make it, I will put in my very best to make sure I pass the Common Entrance with good grade, peradventure I might be given a scholarship by anyone.

She began to study along side with her friend Mary every night; because Mary had all the test books while Adanma did not have any, she took it upon herself, togo to Mary's house with her Lantern and her writing materials to Mary's house every night, there they study overnightcontinuously till the day of the examination.

On the day of the examination, they went to the examination center which was located at the neighboring community, the examination time was scheduled for 8am and students were to be there earlier before 7am.

Mary and Adanma , left their home as early as 5am and hurried by foot to the center of their examination, getting there, they saw other boys and girls from different schools that came to seat for the same exams ,seeing the whole candidates, tension of the exam fever and anxiety gripped Adanma and Mary because they haveseen other children to compete with.

But at the end of the examination, approximate three months after, the result was release by the state education board,Adanma got the highest grade from her school and from among the entire classmates in her community.

Her excellent performance brought jubilationto her family and friends all through the village,it was unbelievable that a daughter of a hunter could be that brilliant,she became the talk of the villagers as a record breaker and many parents used her good result to give examples to their own playful children.

Her Mother and Father became very proud of her, yet they didn't shift ground on their decision and believe that girl child education is a waste of time and resources; still they tried to make her drop her ambition of going to Secondary school.

CHAPTER 14

The new yam festival is an ancient tradition from our ancestral fathers; it is an annual festival of traditional thanks given to God Almightyfor the harvest of each year. The occasion happens always at the 8th months of August yearly among all Igbo Nation,it is a strong cultural heritage that brings the community members together annually, at this period all the illustrious sons and daughters of thatcommunityscarttered abroad, comes home from various cities to celebrate the festival.

aziNwokoma reminded her daughter about the importance of the yearly occasion, and how beautiful girls gets married during the occasion, he said that most married ladies, met their husbands during this occasion, as many young men will return from the cities for the festival and many young people will also come from the neighboring villages and town to our New Yam Festival.

Most of the young men coming, might be comingfor the reason to search for a wife to marry because girls in the city are considered over corrupt, very lazyand thatcannot make good house wife,that's more reasons why young men comes back to village to hunt for pretty girls like my daughter, therefore make up your mind and beautify yourself, peradventures any of them will ask your hand in marriageat this festival period that will be a great blessing to our family.

This got Adanma sad and very worried at her parents persuasion on her to get married at her age while her mates who never got her kind of result were preparing to go to school, this made her, not to eat for many days,she was sad all through crying, remembering thatby September, all her mates and friends will be proceeding to their various posted Secondary Schools, leaving her behind again in the village.

She continued praying to God for help and she refused to give up from her vision and dream., the new yam festival celebration draws nearrer, as it is an occasion done in all Igbo land by all Igbo people from generations to generation; the occasion brings families, friends and community together in harmony and has no idols worship inclinations as people terms it to be.

As the great awaited new yam festival day remaining just 7 days to come, many families were on the lookout, waiting for their Sons, daughters and loved ones returning from various citiesand from various schools.

The village head had given order for the roads and all environmentsto be cleared and kept clean, the town crier came out at night by 8pm during moonlight tales, with his talking drum to announce the village head instructions to the people of the community.

 "Kokom, Kokom, Kokom, kokom, was the sound of the talking drum" and the voice of the town crier was heard saying, everybody listen to me carefully wherever you maybe by this time and listen very well to this announcement from our village head.

I bring the greetings of the village head to you all and his massage, he said as the new yam festivals day is remaining 7 days to come, therefore tomorrow all the young boys and young girls are expected to assemble at the village square for environmental sanitation for onward cleanup of the community and roads by 7am. Because of the new yam festival, anyone that refuses to comeout,shall face the penalty and shall pay a fine of N2000" please pass this message to other people; let no one say, I did not hear." Kokom, Kokom, Kokom.

The nest day, the entire villageyouth's responded to the order and came out in mass, to render their civic responsibility to their community,the boys were with their knives and wrecks, while the girls came out with hoes and brooms,Adanma came out andshe met her friend Mary and other young girls and boys too, Mary was excited to see her friend that she informedAdanma that her parents will soon return for the new yam festivals and to prepare her for the secondary school.

Adanma was glad to hear friends good news but was cold inside her mind because of her uncertain future of going to school, she reminded her friend never to forget her promise to tell her father their plans to spend holidays at Lagos after the new yam festival when he comes, Mary said baby chill I won't forget is in my mind, thanks Adanma said.

Mary said to her, baby thisyear new yam festival would be an interesting occasion, checkout the way every family were preparing for it heavily, I can sense it that many people in the cities are expected by their family members to return home for the festivaland we are going to have real funs, butAdanma, was not expecting any family member of such, because not even a person from her family lives in the city, these made herto be more sad and worried.

 During the festival, there use to be lots of funs like traditional wrestling, Masquerade dances andEdere female dancing concert at the village square.

Visitors from nearby villages troops in to witness the occasion, in laws and friends comes in to the village to celebrate with their relations.

Families will cook different dishes, those that have money will slaughter goats while some other families do contribute money to slaughter cow for the festival and share according to each person financial contributions in their yearly family cooperative meeting

CHAPTER 15

The great day of the New Yam Festival, it was on a Saturday, the entire village was filled with people; family members that came back from the citieswith their children including those that are fromoverseas.

During this festiveseason, businesses owners in the village usually experience buinessbooms at such season and price of commodities rises, those that has shops and restaurants makes quick turn over ofselling, more especially the drinking bars were always filled with people starting from morning hours till night,as men and youths entertains each other with drinks at homes and at different bars, while the women and their children are busy cooking.

The village atmosphere completely changed, because of the occasion, there was different sounds of musics heard coming from various families, children that came from the city were seen riding bicycles with other village children running about with them begging to have a ride, the grown up boys and girls that came from cities were parading about the village showcasing their different hair styles and latest fashionsand swags, having good times together.

One could feel the spirit of the celebration on the air also by perceiving the sweet smelling aroma of foods people are cooking.

People were coming to MaziNwokoma to buy from him his Palm Wine, and he made so many salesand so much Profit also his wife sold her vegetables, red oil, Crayfish and made lots of profits toothat they could cook good food for the occasion.

MaziNwokoma was expecting his in laws, people from his maternal homeand his co palm wine tappers from other villages to come and celebrate the festival with them, but Adanma was not very happy as she noticed that not even one member of her family lives in the city, She was trouble at the level of poverty in her family and she continue to wish herself a better future for her family.

After visitors had come and every one ate and drank, it was about 1pm, people began to move down to the village square for the recreation, already the sound of the masquerade music wasechoing everywhere from the square. Adanma decided to visit her friend Mary first as to move down together to the village square with her.

 Reaching at Mary's house that afternoon, there at the front of the house seated Mary's father who came home with his entire family from Lagos was seating outside in front of his bungalow building with a jug of fresh palm wine and Mary's siblings were playing football outside, while Mary and her mother were in the kitchen frying chicken and preparing salad.

Mary was inside her house and she heard her friendsvoice, she became very happy seeing Adanma came to her house wearing one of the beautiful dress she gave to her.

Adanma greeted Mary's father "Good afternoon Sir" my name is Adanma, I am Mary's friend and classmate I came to see her, Happy New Yam Festival Sir, Mary's father responded "thank you my daughter" you are welcome, but I don't know your father "I am MaziNwokoma first daughter she said.

Oh my daughters you are welcome, how is your father and his beautiful wife?Your father is my friend and my age grade; he is a very good and hardworking man I know him too well, how is he doing, my parents are fine thank you sir.

You are welcome my daughter, let me call your friend for you, "Mary, Mary" yes Daddy Mary responded, come over here, you have a visitor, your friend is here" Mary came out and hugged her friend and said, Daddy this is my friendAdanma the girl I told you about that got the highest grade in the Common Entrance examination and she is interested to come with me to Lagos during the holidays, yes my daughter I have seen her and her father is my friend and age grade, don't worry ,coming to Lagos will never be a big issue if only her parents will permits her.

Mary's father was very glad to see her as a friend to their daughter, Mary take your friend inside and make her feel alright, yes dad Mary responded and took her friend inside to her mother,Adanma was welcomed by Mary's mother, she asked, how are you? What is your name? Adanma answered, I am fine Ma, my name is Adanma, oh my dear you are welcome how are your parents?They are fine Ma, thank you.

Mary's mother told her daughter to offer her friend drink and food, so Mary offered her a bottle of Coca – Cola with rice, Salad and Chicken, but Adanma accepted the soft drink and refused the food, Mary was surprise and not happy, but Adanma said that she had eaten enough food at home before coming out .

 Mary's mother was so surprise at her refusal of the palatable food she was served and persuading her to eat, but she refused the offer, Mary's Mother took a second look at her and respected Adanma the more as a girl that has good home training andself-control.

CHAPTER 16

Immediately Mary and Adanma played down to the village square, still discussing the new life they will face in the Secondary school by September, Mary was very excited as her parents has bought her all books and everything she might need at secondary,butAdanma did not know her faith concerning her going to secondary based on her parent stand.

When they got to the village square, great activities werealready going on as the whole field wasfilled with people, most people appeared on their finesttraditional dresses, and there were manymasquerades running about with their drummers and crowd of people running after them.

 TheEdere dance group was also in the field, made of young beautiful girls performing the female dance that involves shaking of their waist, the dancers had their Shake, Shake on their waist and on their two legs that produces the sounds as they were dancing in lines,theEdere dancing concertis mostly done bythe young girls, so entertaining that every young boys and men likes to watch the girls culturaldance with excitement.

The traditional wrestlers were in their own side warming upfor their contest, entertaining the spectators with power show and demonstrations , so Adanma and her friends also met other of their friends in the market square, they all had real good time running and dancing round the square till evening at the end of the event .

Then the village head announced that the king, the Igwe of the Land His Royal Highness will be addressing the entire community after the occasion, therefore everybody must wait to hear his yearly advise and prayers.

The occasion was over crowded and well attended, it appeared that many families returned for the festival that yearthan other years and the king was very pleased that the event was very peaceful and orderly as each groups participated in their games in turns and the Dike wrestling title of the year was given to the unbeatable young man that won the year wrestling contest.

When the king rose up to speak, a very loud voice of joy from the people celebrating the presence of their king in their midst, the whole people shouted "Igweee!! Igweeee!!!, Igadioooo "Meaning Oh King, oh king, you will Live long" and the king was happy he raised his Kingship Staff up in salute of the crowd, Nsirimokwenu, haaaaa, Igbo kwenuu, haaaaaa,was the people responce, and the king began his address, as he began to speak, there was a great calm and silence, because everybody wanted to hear from the king.

THE IGWE'S ANUAL ADDRESS

Firstly, the king lifted up a cola nut and a glass of dry gin and gave thanks to God Almighty, theChukwuAbiama, meaning the God of Abraham and their ancestors, for sustaining the community throughout the season to see another yearof bountiful harvest which they experienced, he also salute his palace cabinetsmembers for their corporations on good policies they are making to maintain peace in the community and all the Royal Fathers from the other nearby villages that came to celebrates with them, and to all the men and women of the land more especially.

The Ezeji title holders "(The King of yam title holders) , those famers that are great yam farmers he said to them to increase their yam seedlings as to produce more yams next and be ready to crowned the chieftaincy title of EZE JI.

He said. I commended the yam title holders for their hard work and for making sure that there isenough food in the community this season, I askall you farmers to transfer your farming skills to these our younger generations and children, because many of our young men and women are losing interest in farming which is ourcore valuable occupation we are known for.

The king praised the youths in the village, as well as thosethat resides in the city who are contributing for the development of our community, I salute you all,ChukwuAbiama will bless you all, the wealth of the city will not pass you people, the evil in the city, will not come near our children, the people responded Iseyeeeeeeeeeeee

I am very happy and proud of all you patriotic sons and daughters of our great communityNsirimo, more especially for the fact that none of you have brought us shame,and too, thefew of you that remembers to bring your investment home, that is a very wise decision, because we must learn from the bitter experience of Biafra and Nigeria civil war that started in 1967 and ended 1970, where many of us then lost all our propertiesto other regions and states regarded as abandoned properties and we also lost millions of our love ones , may you people not make such a mistakes as we did, by not investing at home, the entire crowd responded ,Iseyeeeeeeeeeeee .

Andmy wish, is for others to emulate from you all and start to do likewise, I pray that our ancestors will not let you people down and the enemy of the roads and the one in the city will not see you people ,the entire crowd responded" Iseyeeeeeeee, .

The king did not forget the young youths in the village, most of them were without any formal education, some are O' Level certificate holders without any helper, some were results awaiting people like Adanma and co, some have leant some trade but no capital to start their trade, in all these, the King express his worries, pointing to the danger of idleness, as the wise people have said, idle mind is a devils workshop, "therefore he pleaded that such people should be assisted to leave the village to the city, he said many have formed criminal gang of smokers , drunkards, rapists and many other bad habits that are not good to be mentioned, characters that are capable of tarnishing the good name of our community out there.

The king appreciated all the youths of the land, he salute all forwell behavedand good characters youths, mostly thoseof you we know that are engaged with one legitmatevocations or the other which you doto help yourselves and families, I pledge to offer my support to any of you when ever my help is needed the king said and the people responded long live our king.

Now I want everyone to listen to my voice, he said, This Year New Yam Festival is a very remarkable one because it was well attended, it is my joyonce again to welcome you all our illustrious sons and daughters who came from the city to celebrate the New Yam Festival with us, I pray when you will be going back to your base, ChukwuAbiama will lead you all back safely and I want you all to always remember that, there is no place like home.

This occasion of new yam festival we have celebrated,did not start today, it is a strong cultural heritage which we inherited from our ancestors,it pains my heart as most religious groups are condemning it and trying to abolish it by attributing it to idol worship which is not true, it is biblically known as Harvest festivals commanded by God.

It is not an idol worship culture, buta yearly event by which we come together to give God thanks for bountiful harvest he gave to us, there is no rituals or idol worship attached to it, this occasion started from the Bible days when Jehovah god asked the Jews people which we the Igbo's are among, to celebrate the harvest, our forefathers handed the culture to us as to brings us together and strengthened the bond of unity, love and for the progress of our land, therefore we must not allow a tradition of this kind to die, rather let your foreign friends know about it and bring them along next time to enjoy our rich culture.

You the abroad basedsons and daughters ,should not forget our land and don't waste your wealth in the city by helping others to develop their countries by those mansions you build there but leaving your fathers land as desolate, bring your investments nearer home, we have enough land that is capable to accommodate every investment and buildings.

It is time for us to think of bringing electricity to our community and to dig one or two bore holes to make water available in our community, we don't have drinking water; this will help ease the sufferings of our people if you all team up for the project, it will be achieved.

I want more cooporations among all our young people both those at home and those living in the cities, for more progress to come to our land, all our youths that are through with their academics or apprenticeship training that are roaming about in the villagejoblessly, shouldfind a way to leave the village to the city through the help of you their Uncles and Aunties that are already in the cities, because there are no white collar jobs or business here in the village.

Finally, I am very happy at the good results of our sons and daughters who did very well in the just concluded Common Entrance Examination and those that did very well in the last West African Examination Council (WAEC) examination, more especially those candidates that got higher grades.

Therefore, as the King of this Kingdom of our great land, I am declaring that such people should be given scholarship to continue with their education so as to do our community more proud, we need to produce our own indigenous qualified medical Doctors, Lawyers, Pilots, Police, Solders, Customs officers, Big business men and women etc for our community.

Therefore he said, as the King of this land, all those that passed this year Common Entrance with good grade, will receive scholarship from their year one to their final year in the secondary school, courtesy of the king and the community cooperatives.

Also, those that passed very well from the college, shall receive scholarship to University courtesy of the community contributions and the King royal support, the whole crowd began to scream for joy, hailing the name of their king "Igweeeeee!!!Igweeeeee, Igweeeeeeeeee, long live our king and the drummers gave him a short sweetmasquerade interlude to appreciate him.

The palace secretary was standing beside the king holding the palace register containing the names of beneficiaries of the kings scholarship scheme, carefully compiled by merit, so among thelist was,AdanmaNwokoma whose name wasthe first on the kings list to be mentioned.

Everybody began to listen attentively as palace secretary opened his registerand called the first name and it was,ADANMA NWOKOMA. People began to clap their hands as she was called out from the great crowd to come forward for identification and to receive her scholarship letter, these was a great surprise to her, hearing her name first among all , very unexpected to everyone,she burst into crying as she was coming out to the platform, many people where happy and surprise at her expression, some held their mouth, some lifted their hands on their head knowing whose daughter she was, Mary'sfather and mother who were also among the crowd, was amazed and eager to hear whose name shall be next maybe their daughter.

CHAPTER 17

Adanmathe poor girl was just crying while the king was making his remarksspeech about her performances as everybody were waiting to see her step forward to the platform to receive her scholarship award letter.

Reaching the platform, she knelt down before the king still crying, the king was moved emotionally that he gave a very good remarks about her character and he said he would be glad seeing her doing better at secondary school throughout her stay till the end.

The king said, onbehalf of our community and my palace cabinet, we offer you this 6years scholarshipthroughout your secondary school, we shall bear the 100% percent cost of your studies, all we expect from you is to maintain this good result till the end, then he presented the award letter to her as she stretched forth her two hands to receive from the king the scholarship award letter.

the king said to her stand up my daughter, she stood with the letter given to her before the entire village, her Mother and Father were speechless and their eyes filled with tears of joy sayingChukwuDaalu, "Meaning Thank God"ChukwuAbiama you are indeed God of the poor and of those that put trust in you, you have granted the wish of our daughter her dream has come through, while his wife was dancing, jubilating with tears of joy, Adanma fall to her knees thanking God for listening to her prayers.

At the end of the occasion, they all got home, it was a night of jubilation for MaziNwokoma family as Adanma was dancing all through, given thanks to God for answering her prayers, saying my dreams has come through.

That night, she began to give hope and promises to her parents and to her sibling saying, after my secondary school, I will gain admission into the university to study medicine so as to become a medical doctor to take care of our family and the entire community.

MaziNwokoma was siting outside receiving cool breeze that night, he was relaxing with a jar of Palm Wine, having his box of snuff which he is holding by his left hand, while his wife was busy preparing for him his Favorite dish, it was a well celebrated festival for us he said, as God has crowned it for us with answers to our daughter's prayers.

As the days goes by, Adanma began her preparations for leaving for secondary school as in reality, the Igwe the King through the village head, sent to her some amount of money for the purchase of sandals, school box, textbooks and other things she might need, her mother was busy arranging for her some food items like rice, beans, yams, garri, red oil, salt crayfish etc which she must take to school.

Adanma became happierwhen the Admission letter came via the post office, the post master brought it to her, and shewas posted to a very nice School together with her friend Mary.

CHAPTER 18

It was like a day dream to her, as the new academic section resumed that September and she was among the new set of girls that left the village for college.

The night before the very day she left for school, her mother was troubled at how she might cope at school without her parents. "She said AdanmaNwam "Meaning My daughter, don't forget the promises you made to us, don't allow anything to stop you half way, choose the good kind of friends to keep, don't be misled by those good for nothing boys out there in the school that has no future plan than to drink, smoke and cause troubles.

Mammaaa, stop saying that over other people children, besides I know myself and what I want from life, don't be afraid about me, and the mother said again, remember thatIgwe our king and the villagers will not forgive you if you disappoint them tomorrow please my daughter make use of this opportunity to better your life, the moment her mother madethat statement, Adanma became calm and looked at her mother's eye to eye "The statement was like an iced water poured into a glass cup that produces instant chills, immediately Adanma smiled and looked up to heaven and said to her mother, God will help me.

The same time,MaziNwokoma called upon her and said, I don't have much to tell you because your mother has said it all, the proverb said, a wise child is the one that listened to the advice of the parents and do what they said, but the foolish child throws away such advice of parents and do otherwise.

 As you are going to college, remember it is God that made it possiblefor you, please focus on your studies, be a good girl you have always been, don't go to college to learn bad character, remember evil communication, corrupts good manners, I will not receive you into this house if youreturn with pregnancy, follow your mothers good step which I have told you time without number that she was a virgin till her 18 years before I married her, I prayto God of our land to keep you from all evils and help you there "Adanma said Amen.

Meanwhile Adanma and her friend Mary had concluded plans to leave for school the same day, therefore at thebreak of the day, Adanma picked up her box and bags as everybody in the family bid her good bye and farewell., she walked down to Mary's house happily and theyboth arrived at the school, it was a very big school that has a lot of class rooms, principal office, teachers staff room, teachers resident quarters, female dormitoryand male dormitory, big football field for games, sciencelibratory, refectory, school book shop and garden etc.

The school compound was so large that the junior section was one side while the senior section was at the other side and the population of the students was so much that she was marvelled seeing the college setting.

Adanma discovered that many of the students came from various cities and most of them could hardly speak vernacular because they born and brought up in the city, but she was not moved by that, rather she began to practice speaking in English, trying to improve her communication skill, it became more tasking to her when the English master made it a law of the school that vernacular communication except during the vernacular subject period remains prohibitedin the school , he said serious punishment awaits offenders.

Adanma became very careful in chosen friends as she was always found reading and doing her assignment, while Mary met other girls and boys that joined the school from various cities like, Lagos, Kano state, Poracourt , etc. Mary chosen to made friends with such people because she considered them to have been more exposed than Adanma.

Gradually Mary began to withdraw her closeness with Adanma, not keeping that cordial relationship as usual, now Mary with her newfriends began to attenddisco parties at weekends, having no more time to study with Adanma as usual,Adanma was very surprised at Mary's new character at school towards her, but she kept hearing and rememberingher mother's advice, never to be deceived by the good for nothing students at school.

CHAPTER 19

From the year one to her final year in the college, Adanma maintained her academicperformances standard, scoring first position in class at all examination and she became the overall best studentcharacter wise and academically.

The news of her excellent performance got to the hearing of the king, he was very pleased that he began to make arrangement for her scholarship extension to "(Mahadum)"University;peradventure she could pass her WAEC very well.

The king was veryhappy at the feedback he wasgetting from the beneficiaries of the community scholarship scheme, more especially that of Adanmas excellent behaviors and her seriousness at her studies, therefore the king summons an emergency meeting of his cabinet chiefs, seeing how excited the king was, one among the kings cabinet asked to know what is causing the kings gladness of heart this time, maybe the king has received gift of money from the local government chairman, who knows if he gathered us to share it with us.

The king responded to his council of chiefssaying, my joy is coming from the feedback reports reaching me from the excellent performances of the beneficiaries of our community scholarship scheme, more especially the excellent performances reports from that little daughter of MaziNwokomawhom our community gave scholarship through our revenue to secondary school, her report of excellent performances at school is so satisfactory to me that has been my joy.

Therefore I called this meeting to seek the opinion of you my cabinet members on my consideration to extendingAdanma scholarship to the higher institution, saying we should not allow such a brilliant girl to stop halfway, furthering her education, will indeed do this community proud in future the king said.

Theking's suggestion came to the ear of most the chiefs, like sand in the delicious cooked rice in the mouth of the eaters, and the king said it would notbe a bad idea if we consider offering her a complete help to furthering her education courtesy of our community, one among the chiefs rose and asked "Igweee, tell us ofwhat benefit would these your suggestionbring to our community if we buy to it.

These your suggestions did not go down well with me in particular, knowing too well that girls child education is a waste of time and resources, besides perhapsafter sponsoring her at the end she mightgets married tomorrow to a far community or country as the case maybe then all we have done would be like water purred in a basket.

Tell us what will be our benefits if we continue to sponsor her to high institution?Calmdown chiefAkudo, the Igwe responded, every girl child should be given equal opportunity like their male counterparts in education despite the fact that the child in question is not our biological child that should not stop us from completing the good gesture we started.

Many communities have benefited immensely from their trained girl children who grew up and got married to prominent non indgens outside their state, some got married to governors, presidents and successful business men that are far away, yet through them great development came from their in-laws simple because of their well trained daughters.

Have you forgotten that our daughter Mrs.Mary Peter Odili the wife of former Governor of River State is our daughter from Imo state but married to river state man who later became a governor, what about latechief Mrs. Stella Obasanjo, from Delta state who got married to the former president of the Federal Republic of Nigeria, and late Chief Miriam Babangida, our daughter from Delta state but got married to the former head of state from Niger state.

All these were females children from other States that married far away from their state, just to mention but a few, therefore I have the convision that educating a girl child opens more opportunity and give better hope forfamilies and communities.

 GOD has blessed our community with a very brilliant girl that can replicate history ofsuch blessing to our community tomorrow, I am very pleased with her performances at school, which the principal gladly informed me when I enquired about her, infarct I was told that she remains the most brilliant girl in the entire school and the most well behaved among other girls and boys.

That girlchild of a poor hunter, is a blessing to our community, she deserves our communitysupport, some among the chiefs replied, why should she be our subject of discursions and argument?A daughter of an ordinary hunter and Palm Wine Tapper.

 And the King said "That is the very reason why you should consider my plea on her behalf to extend her scholarships to Mahadum of higher learning (University), as to help her poor parents.

,instantly some members of the King's cabinet reacted to it and said it is not advisable and you will not get our vote on that because we all have our own children to train at that moment one among them rose up to move motion for adjournment and the meeting ended without any positive result.

The king asked why? They said it will be a waste of venture because she is not a male child that will remain herewith us to develop our community; she will get married tomorrow to another community, then what shall be our gain?.

The argument brought discouragement to the King's heart, meanwhile; Adanma has become the center of attraction in the school and her entire community because of her intelligence and sound morals.

CHAPTER 20

It was her fourth year in secondary school, all her siblings have gone to various cities to learn different vocations by the help of other village relatives residing in the cities, Adanma came home to meet only his father and mother living alone at home; her parents were so delighted to welcome her back from college.

Adanma went straight toher mother's kitchen in search of food to eat after which she went straight to the kings palace to pay homage andgreetings to the king, getting to the palace, there the king was on a meeting with other traditional rulers from other communities, when the king sighted Adanma standing by the Corner of the palace door, the king was happy that he sent the palace guards to call her in, and as she came in, she went straight on her knees down before the king and she said long live our king, long live your kingdom , and the king placed on her shoulder his handy fan made of horse tail, and he said you are welcome my daughter, rise up and she arose.

The king was pleased tointroduce her before his fellow traditional rulers, telling them of the scholarship scheme which his kingdom gave to some youths whichthis girl standing before us here today is a living beneficiaries of that gesture, hearing that every one clapped their hands for king andAdanma received blessings from the Royal father's and she joined the ushering group in serving the guests till the meeting was over and the King ordered the cook to arrange a take home food and gift items for her and she was asked to revisit the palace before leaving back to school, and she went on her knees, thanked the king and the royal fathers andshe left.

Adanma got back home, handed all she was given to her mother , who was amazed seeing thesurprised package she brought home from a very caring king.

The mother could not hide her joy and she prayed, may he continue to reign over us as our king, and may his children children be highly favored by God and men wherever they may be, and she took the basket of all that Adanma brought from the king to her husband and he was glad also that he blessed the King the more.

During the holidays, Adanma helped her mother so much at home, both in cooking, and farming, and most times she followed her mother to the big market that holds every four days,and each time on their wayto that market, shewill never passed any adult without offering greetings to the person unlike other youths of the community.

Many people took notice of that good quality of her, and developed interest and more likeness on her, some parents would even wish their son to marry her, most times, some mothers do send her gift items such as fruits and other items.

One day during the holidays, Adanmavisited her Maternal home to be with her grandmother and grandfather atthe other community across the river; there shewas able to make new friends, although her grandmother was a very strict and disciplinarian woman, that does not allow too many visitors in her house especially opposite sex friendship.

Adanma spent some days at the maternal home and she enjoyed so much love and care from her grandparents who also advised her to put more efforts and concentration on her studies, never to be misled by any person, after that she came back home with lots of food items that were given to her and withsome amount of pocket money given to her by her grandparents.

Reaching to her father's compound, hermother has gone to farm while her father was at home under the cola nut tree where he was plating his raffia roofing sheet, seeing her daughter,MaziNwokoma was very glad he welcomed her happily, enquiring from her about her grandfather and grandmother, they are fine she said, "Papa, grandmother gave me all these items and grandfather also gave me some money, they were very happy with me, that's too kind of them he said, may God bless them.Ameeeeen!!! Adanma responded.

Where is Mama she asked? your mother has gone to the nearby farm to harvest some cassava for us to have some food at home and for the market tomorrow, she might be on her way coming back, Papa let me go to meet her, immediately she left her father running down to the farm to meet her mother, getting closer to the farm, behold her mother coming carrying on her head a basket full of cassava, her mother saw her coming running down towards the farm.

Adanma are you back?And you came searching for your mother; only you by this lonely time, don't you know that there are bad people in this village and dangerous animals in the bush? You are supposed to wait for me at home, Adanmaresponded, "Mama I can't wait at home, doing what? While you are at the bush only you,Mama let me carry the basket, so the mother transferred the basket on her head and she carried the basket home, people who saw her, were praising her and calling her good daughter and her Mother was proud of her.

At home Adanmanarrated to her mother all she enjoyed at her maternal home and she brought out all the items her grandparents gave to her, Adanma said to her mother, I pray to God to keep them alive till I am through with my schooling, I will take them to the city, may God answer your prayers my daughter, iseeeeeeeeeeeeeeee.

Adanma told the mother, Mama I will be revisiting the palace, because the king required my coming back to the palace before going back to school by the end of the holidays, OdinmaAdamm the mother responded , meaning it is a good idea to revisit the kings palace, maybe this time, we need to go with you so as to appreciate the king for all his kindness extended to our family.

 Mama that will be nice if we go together, it is good for people to say thank you to people that doesgood or any help to them, that is what our teacher thought us, he called it gratification and appreciation.

The next day,Adanmas mother notified her husband about their daughters second visit to the palace as demanded by the king, and I feel it would be good of us to accompany our daughter to the palace as to appreciate the king for all he has been doing to our family, MaziNwokoma applauded the idea and promised to join in the visit, and he said to the wife, but remember no one visits the king with empty hands without a gift, that is true my husband what can we give to a rich man that he can appreciate? She asked.

 He has a enough in the palace, it is not about the quantity or the amount of gift one can give, what the rich people appreciate is your mind and sense of gratitude, he added that gifts given to the rich are powerful keys that can open anyclosed door of blessing, therefore whatever we can afford at our reach shall be acceptable.   That's true my husband, that means we should go there with whatever we have, yes but something worth given to a king, that will not tell bad of our family, therefore Obidiya , go and prepare one full gallon of red oil and I will arranged one 25 Liters of fresh palm wine, with these we can visit the king, yes my husband.

The nest day, they set for the visit, MaziNwokoma brought out the Palm wine and his wifearranged 10 Liters of red oil,Adanma carried the palm wine as they move to the king's palace,

At the kings palace, MaziNwokoma and his family was welcomed honorably as the king expressed his surprises and gratitude for their visit, he said I never expected these whole family surprising visit to my palace today, but I am happy for the visit, it speaks volume of your pure heart of gratitude towards the sacrifice of the community to your family, once again, is my pleasure and my joy to welcome   you MaziNwokoma and your highly respected wife, the daughter of my friend , the traditional village head of Obizi Community in Nbaise, you are welcome to my palace.

MaziNwokoma stood up and thanked the king and his cabinet for the scholarship scheme which his daughter is one among the beneficiary, he said my family will foreverremains gratefulto these kind gestures of the king, may you reign forever, and may our chukwuAbiama prolong your days on earth in Jesus name Amen, and everyone in the palace responded Iseeeeeeeeeeeeeeeeeeeeee.

The king received from them the gift of palm wine and presented it tohis people to drink, while they were drinking, the king expressed his profound joy over the performance's of Adanma at school and her exemplary good behavior in this village which everybody are testifying about, at the end the king blessed her and handed to her an envelope containing her school fees and to buy books and her final examination registration fees and the family stood up and thanked the king and left the palace back home.

Now Adanma began her preparation to return back to school as the end of the holiday's draws closer, the mother began to arrange food items that she might be in need of at school, also her father gave herpocket money from the amount he has saved from his farm produced and from his Palm wine.

The night to the day she was to return back to school, her mother as usual sat her down and continued to advice her and praying for her, Adanma was happy because the holidays has come to an end she will be going back to school to reunite with her class mates and friends also to continue with her study because the WAEC examination was fast approaching.

It was on Sunday afternoon after church service, that she picked up her bags ready to leave back to school, her father kept her standing, and he said to her, my daughter listen to my words carefully, put more efforts and seriousness in your studies and to alwaysremember your siblings when my God blesses you, look at yourmother make sure that she does not suffer, Yes Papa I have heard and I will take care of you also, I don't understand why all these statements she said.

 These are my few words to you for now, no one knows tomorrow, may the gods of our fathers be with you as you go back to school, she responded iseeeeeeeeeeeeee.Adanma been a little girl does not know that the advice of his father was his last parting words to her forever as the first daughter of the family.

Adanma was happy living home for school, promising to be back again during midtermbreak and she left by foot to the market where she could easily join a taxi going to the town.

CHAPTER 21

It was the first termin new academic session of her final year after a long holidays period, all students were very eager to get back to school as to reunite with their classmates and friends, Adanma arriving at school, she went to the female hostel to check on her friend Mary and others, she could not find Mary because Mary was yet to return from Lagos where she went to spend the holidays with her parents.

Adanma could not find many of her classmates, as she went back to her out of schoolrented accommodation where she resides; she began her usual study ahead of others because WAEC examination was ahead of them, she was offering sciences, having it in mind to study medicine or petrochemical engineering in the university.

The school had resumed three weeks past and Mary was yet to returne from Lagos, Adanma was imagining in her heart how Mary could cope, having missed most lectures, just as she was thinking about her friend, behold the taxi that brought Mary back to school emerged at the school gate, the taxi wasstopped by the security guard at the gate for interrogations and clearance.

Mary brought out her student identity card, showed it to the guard, who then allowed the Taxi car drove into the school compound, as it arrived carrying Mary and her luggage's, her anxiously awaiting friends saw her highlighting from the Taxi, they all with joy ran to her to welcome her and helping her carry her traveling bags to the hostel.

Adanma expressed great joy seeing her friend come back to school from her Lagos holidays trip, and Mary indeed saw the joy and excitement in her friend as they were shouting " Mary,Mary my baby, the Lagos Chic, you are welcome" Mary replied " Ada baby my Darling girl, what's up, how are you, ? When did you returned to school?

Adanma said" It was a day before resumption date that I breezed in"

Mary said.Aaaaah why so early?

Adanma replied , yes it was because the long vacation was too long that I got tired of staying at the village, moreover I didn't want to miss any lectures from the beginning of this term"

 Mary said, that was nice my serious girl, you mean you didn't had funs during this holidays all you were thinking was to rush back to school?As for me, nothing would have made me resume that early, there was so much funs at Lagos withguys.

So they both walked down to the femalehostel,Adanmacarrying one of Mary's bags, reaching at the hostel, Mary brought out packets of biscuit and sweet candy's she bought from Lagos, she shared to all friends and they all ate from it, other friends where coming to welcome Mary back to school, and she also shared to them the gifts she brought back from Lagos.

Adanma spent much time with Mary as they were gossiping to each other about all that happened during the holidays.

Mary was interested asking about guys in the village that returned from other schools for holidays, was there any disco parties stagedatcentral school hall during the holidays?

Adanma responded. I wouldn't know, of course there would be, like you know before now that I am not the party type, such are not my priority for now, but as for guys, many of them were around and many did asked about you from me.

Mary asked. Who and who did ask of me and what did you tell them?

Adanma replied. Nne, I told them you are fine at Lagos, having your good time alone over there hence you refused taken me along to Lagos as you promised.

Mary replied. I trust you my babe, but how could I have taken you to Lagos when all the time till this your age you have refused socializing neither have you met any guy before.

Adanma said to her. Mary you fail to understand that my case is like the case of one sitting on one chance opportunity that I must not joke with till I get to my destination, however I know you must be very hungry by now, let's go down to my room , I have some food for us to eat.

Really, Mary asked?Yes my dear, Adanma said,sothey left to her outside school resident where she is sharing a room with a classmate at a building opposite the school compound.

CHAPTER 22

Few weeks later after resumption, the sudden ugly news of Adanmafather's ill health got to her hearing from the principal who received the message from the king's palace messenger that brought the letter from the king to the principal, requesting for immediate release of Adanma to see her very sick father.

The principal broke the news to her privately and she became disturbed, restless and surprise at hearing that her father's health is in critical condition, knowing that there was no money to care for her sick father medically.

Quickly she got the school authority approval and she hurried home from the school the next day, having told her friend Mary and others, with the principal permission. As she arrived the community, getting closer to her father's compound, she began to notice unusual movements of peopletrooping in, in her father's compound.

Quickly she could sensed that something has gone wrong in the family as each person were comingout soberly with their arms folded to their chest, the mood of the people she was seeing was coming out sent a signal to her mind that all was not well.

Looking up straight to her compound from afar, she saw people holding her mother who was sitting on the floor crying and surrounded by otherwomen that was consoling her.

Her mother sighted her coming, she threw herself on the ground, shoutingand crying Adanmaeeeeeee, Adanmaeeeeee (NnagiAwungooooooo) meaning your father has died.

 The young girl rushed down to her mother, flung away her bag, grabbed her mother and rushed inside their inner room only to meet her late father lying in state she began shouting crying 'Papa, Papa, Papa, what happened answer me , Papa Papa, wake up, somebody tell me, what happened to papa? Oh God why now? Papa you could not wait to see me before leaving us, why Papa wakes up, O God, why now!! She was asking God people were holding her in consolation, many people where coming for condolence from every families.

After few days,the burials arrangement was fixed on a Saturday, preparation was made, as the family members and elders met to plan for his burial, women contributed food items, youths were fetching water, other people brought firewood's, because late MaziNwokoma was nice to everyone, both old and young people mournedhis earlydeath at the age of 59 years.

On his burial day, his hunters association, his palm wine tappers association, his in-laws and his maternal home people all was present, the king and chiefs were there and the village Catholic Church priest and his members, all were present as the priest gave the burial sermon and prayers before he was lowered to the mother earth.

The family cried, Adanma and all her siblings who also returned from their various cities for their late father burial, they all cried holding their mother who never wanted to stop weeping, as she was saying she would die with his husband because of the love they both shared.

After the man was buried, people ate and drank and everyone dismissed to their various home's and after few days Adanma returned back to school for preparation to write her Final examination in the Secondary School, while the most younger child was made to stay behind with their widow lonely mother for few weeks.

CHAPTER 23

As she return back to school, having her hair scrappeddown to her skulls,together with a piece of black cloth pinned to her dress according to Igbo culture as an honor to her Late Father,

.

At school, all her classmates, friends and teachers were coming for condolence to share her sorrows with her and consoling her, but she did not see her best friend Mary, she waited for a day or two without seeing her, she was surprised and worried why her childhood friend from the same community could not visit her to share her sorrows with her.

Soshe went looking for Mary at the female hostel, meeting other friends and classmates, she was told that Mary was rushed to the Clinic for an emergency treatment, Adanma was shocked and curious to know what happened to her friend?, Did she had an accident? She asked.

She was directed to meet Mary at Victoria Hospitalwhere she was admitted; quickly she ran down to the Clinic and found her girlfriend lying almost lifeless on a sick bed, surrounded by the nurses.

Adanma grabbed her by her hands, and she called on her, Mary, Mary is me Adanma talk to me, Mary what's the matter with you? What brought youhere? Mary could not open hereyes and mouth to speak and the Nurses excused Adanma out from the ward tothe reception room, so Adanma waited for a long time and left the hospital and went back to school very worried.

 Not knowing what has happened to her friend and how she can help her, until other friends told her that Mary nearly died of abortion, they said when Mary discovered that she was pregnant as she returned from holidays and she began a secret arrangement's trying to terminate the pregnancy before it became known and visibleto the school.

She consulted a friend of hers, who promised to keep the secret and to take herto a local medicine man that specialized on local herbs for abortion,

Mary and her friend's sneak out of the school to meet the traditional medicine man who prepares veryhot abortionconcortin for the girls of the school to abort theirpregnancy.

Mary hearing about the man and hisConcortion, and she asked "how much will that cost?

Her friend said to her, as much as your school fees which was N25000 Naira.

Mary asked,you mean it will cost that much?

Yes as much as that, or do you want to keep the pregnancy?

 Mary replied, God forbid, my parents will kill me if they happen to know or hear that I am pregnant.

Her friend told her to get set that by weekend they shall visit the local medicine man at the next village, meanwhile Mary's friend had made arrangement behind her for 10 percent commission from the abortion fee charged as agents to the traditional doctor.

Adanma was so astonished and perplexedat what she was hearing and she asked, did Mary pay that much in other to get rid of her unwanted pregnancy?After the payment what next happened?

These was all we knew about her story until the day Mary began to scream in her hostel " my tummy, my tummy,somebody help me I am dying " the whole female students gathered at her room, trying to manage the situation and it continue getting worst, at that time the whole school became aware including the principal and teachers, then she was rushed to the nearby hospital .

There the Doctor and his Nurses said she drank a mixture of harmful chemicals and herbs mixed with strong alcohols substance for abortion, which turned out to destroy her intestinal organs that would have caused her death.

Hearing this,Adanma was mad at Mary, you mean all these happened to her; yes it was too hot and harmful that she would have diedwhen she fainted and collapse, before she was brought to the clinic.

Adanma began to cry for her friend, begging God to save her life, the next day she bought some oranges and apples and went back to the hospital, yet Mary was still in coma as she could not still talk or make movement, the doctors were very kind and experienced, they paid attention on her closelyuntil she was revived back to life after many days, but yet the pregnancy was still with her as the doctor said.

And after few days, Mary's mother arrived from Lagos as the school authority did telegrammed her parents telling them about the ugly incident that happened to their daughter at school, also the principal invited the police for the arrest of the traditional medicine man.

Mary's mother hearing the news, the following day, she boarded the next available transport from Lagos down to Abia State the eastern region to meet her daughter in the hospital, as she arrived to the school, she walked down to the principal office to hear from the school authority about all that happened.

She was directed by the principal with a covering note to see the doctor for better explanation and to pay the hospital bills, she was very angry and highly disappointed at Mary her daughter, as she got to the hospital, she met Adanma at the hospital been the only friend of Mary that stood by her at her sick bed, Mary's motherwas so glad seeing Adanmabeside her sick friend that she thanked her so much before she went into the doctor's office to see the doctor.

AfterAdanma narrated the whole story about all she was told that happened to her friend, Mary's mother also consoled Adanma over the death of her father, she gave her some money as they left the hospital together and went to the principal office, to thanked the school for their kind gestures that saved her daughter from dying

The principal expressed her dismayed and disappointment over the loosed lifestyle the little girl was exposed to by the parents, that made her to become pregnant at a very minor age of 16 years, more painfully at this time her mates are studying hard preparing for their final examination that was fast approaching.

Mary's mother was short of words and very ashamed of her as she realized that it was their fault for leaving the young girl to herself alone in the village without parents.

So she picked Mary's bags and books and left back to Lagos, that was how Mary dropped out from school without completing her Secondary Education.

She became an emergency mother of a boy child, her parents were so disappointed and disgraced, Adanma wrote the WAEC and made all her papers with 7As, and she came back with the best result in the whole community, the news was everywhere,Adanma was very happy and grateful to God and people celebrated her in the whole village, both the king was very pleased with her that he personally promised to render more help to her when the need arises.

CHAPTER 24

After the college, Adanma remained at the village not having anyone in the city that she could call upon for help or to stay with, at this time all her mates who passed out from the college the same year have all traveled out of the village to one city or the other, some have gotten admission into higher institutions furthering their education.

This was another traumatic situation for Adanma, not knowing what next and which direction to follow; knowing that the community had withdrew their support on her, simple because she was a female child that might get married outside their community tomorrow without looking back.

Adanma remains at the village with her widow mother, she was offered a teaching appointment in one of the private owned Nursery and Primary school; there she was made to handle the upper primaries on English language and other science subjects she was very good at, including physical education on games of sports, she was loved by all kids and all students as everyonefondly call her "Aunty Ada"

One day, her mother sat her down trying to convince her to accept suitors that were coming from all villages asking for her hands in marriage,Adanma was19 yearsold then,still a virgin.

During her days in the secondary school, many boys were interested to date her, but she never paid attention to any, this made her to become a highly respected girl both at school and in her community.

Adanma told her mother respectfully, mama I have no other agenda in my mind than to further myeducation to Higher Institution,the mothersaid to her, my daughter who will bear the responsibility? Is it a widow like me?, the mother retorted and asked her in a very cool manner?

Have you forgotten that the village head has been discouraged by his cabinent members and by the community to withdraw the scholarship he promised you to higher institution?

Because they don't believe in a girls childeducation and expecialy when it happens to be a poor girl like you, they considered it to be a waste of time and resources training a woman that will marry and leave the community tomorrow to an unknown village or state.

Adanma did not give up to her dream, she remains focus and full of determination to pursue her dream, in other to achieve the target she set to herself, because she is fighting to change the story of her family for good when she grows up.

She also remembered her response to her mother when she wanted to discourage her from thinking of going to Secondary School, "God will pay my school fees" she began to cry again to God, thanking God for sponsoring her in Secondary School and she was saying "Oh God, I want to school more. I don't want to stop halfway and I don't want to get married now at this age without good education, I want to become a medical doctor so I can help my people, O God help me, she was crying and praying.

Her mother walked into the room where she was, and she asked,Adamm "what's it is again that you would not allowsomebody to hear word in this house?" You know your father is late, how do you want me to do it? Are you the only girl that is brilliant that did not further her education to Mahadum? I have told you to get married now you are very fresh and young, maybe your husband may train you further yet you refused my ideas, stop disturbing my peace.

Adanma did not utter a word to her mother, in other words, she understood the position of her Widow Mother, but in her mind she refused to drop her ambition of schooling. Few weeks later, she made a step forward by introducing her pet project that brought an open door to her.

She thought of the mistake of Mary as something that could happen to any young girl, she decided to introduce girls mentoring program in the community for the young girls as an NGO she called Descent Girls Foundation, (DGF).

During this period,Adanma was going from house to house talking to young girlsteaching them to embrace right moral's and sex education, she also committed her time to God attending all her church prayer meetings and Bible studies, as she kept her self more busy with all these.

This made her more popular in the village, more people got to love her and was given her gifts based on the testimonies coming fromtheir radical daughters that are changing to good girl's, Yet no one was interested to help her push on with her educational dreams.

One day she said to herself, "I will make it, and if I do, I will establish a help foundation to help the poorer youths in our community to achieve their dreams.

Adanma continued to go from house to house advising the young people to follow the new life of the Lord and to remain focus with their education and avoid living life that is capable todestroy their destiny, the story of her friend Mary was like a case study for all.

Chapter 25

Adanma met her age mate that came back from Lagos, she was her childhood girl friend that taken to Lagos as house helpafter their primary school graduation by name Ngozi , that had no opportunity to school beyond primary six and she left for Lagos through her aunt that has a restaurant in Lagos..

As they met again after their first meeting at the village square celebration of the new yam festival year's back, this timeNgozi came back as grown up big girl from Lagos,Adanma was very glad seeing her and they hugged each other.

Ngozi said to her, Adababy, I had you made it brilliantly at WAEC, which university are youright now?"Sheasked,

Adanma replied, my sister I have been at home doing nothing since after my WAEC, no one is willing to help me out, I am wasting away here in the village and my mother is persuading me to get married, I am just fade up of everything.

Ngozi said, I am very surprise to hear all these, I thought the king offered you scholarship up to university?

Adanma responded, yes baby the king did promised but later on he was brainwashed by other kinsmen to withdrew from his promise.

Why that, Ngozi asked? baby I can't explain why, Adanmareplied, all I know was I did my best to pass my exams with very good result, and all my expectations was to continue with schooling courtesy of the kings pronounced scholarship, but unfortunately for me, therevise becomes the case, because people said I am a girl child that need not to be trained up to university by community effort, with the reason that I will get married tomorrow maybe far away from the community, that's all.

Ngozi was sad and very sorry at such disappointment from his kinsmen to a very bright daughter like Adanma, and then she asked Adanma, would you mind following me to Lagos?

Adanma responded immediately, yes my sister that has been my prayer all these while, I will go with you.

Ngozi said , okay get ready we shall leave together by weekend on Saturday to be précise , but bear it in mind that Lagos is not an easy place to stay, things are very though and expensive over there.

Adanma said, but looking at you Ngozi, you look very nice and big, are you working or schooling?My dear is not easy at Lagos; we are just managing over there doing girls runs.

Over there is 100% better than staying in this village Adanma said, her friend promised to take her to Lagos if she cares to come over.

Adanma became very happy and she said "God has heard my midnight cries at last. "And her friend told her "to get ready, five days from now we shall be leaving for Lagos, Young pretty girl like you need not to end up her in thevillage, just get your things ready I will pay your fear and feeding till we get there and I will accommodate you in my little apartment at Lagos till you find a job.

Adanma got home, and break the news to her mother about the big opportunity God has created for her, She said "Mama, I have a good news to share with you, the mother said Adanma My daughter, what is the good news all about, have you met a rich man that have asked your hand in marriage?

 She said to her mother, not that, but I will be going to Lagos next week; her mother shouted and she asked her, "Who do you know in Lagos that you are going to meet there?Do you want them to use you for money rituals? Adanma sat down and narrated the story to her mother and added, this has been the opportunity I have been waiting for, and when I get there I will work and send money to you and buy you fine clothes with wrappers.

Anyway it is a good idea, but I was thinking maybe you have met a man that will marry you because that is the only good news I am waiting to hear.

 From that moment, Adanma kept dreaming and thinking about Lagos, She said when I get to Lagos I will not allow any man to get closer to me, I've heard so much about them, the way they deceive girls and make mess of them, I can never forget what the Lagos boys did to my friend Mary that ended her educational career half way and she became an emergency mother.

WhenI get to Lagos, I will just get work, earn salary and return back to school, I pray to make it big in Lagos she said.

Adanma had prepared to leave for Lagos the next few days, having arranged her bags and baggage's, she has packed her cloths and her certificate into her trunk box waiting for that day she will be leaving the village to the big and beautiful city of Lagos.

Two days more, her troubled mother continue gathering fruits, and she continues to pray for her success and for good husband at Lagos, Adanma really lived a life whort emulating, at 20 years she was still a virgin, no man from their village or nearby village can claim having any carnal knowledge of her, this earned her a lot of reputation and respect in the village, also before her friends.

Adanma visited her friend Mary who was nursing her baby boy whose name shecalled "Hope" Mary, I will be leaving the village next tomorrow for Lagos, Mary was very glad to hear that, she said as soon as I am through with this problem, I will come to Lagos to stay so when you get to Lagos, please visit my parents at 10, Olufowobi StreetLawanson, Surulere, Lagos, please beg my parents on my behalf, Adanma said that is not a big deal as soon as I get to Lagos I will send you a letter, that's fine, says Mary. Both spent sometime and share some old school life storries and Adanma left for her home to prepare for her journey.

CHAPTER 26

The night before the morning she was to leave for Lagos, her mother called her for a talk of advice and prayer, she said "Adanma, I have a question to ask you, what is it Mama? That your friend you are traveling with,Is she born again? Her mother asked, Adanma said 'yes' she is a very kind and nice girl that prays very well. the mother asked her again "but what is she doing at Lagos? Is she working in the Bank?

Adanma replied,Maaama, I don't know, but I know she is okay andshe lives alone and she is helping her family very well. Aaaaaaaaah she lives alone at Lagos? She must be a prostitute, the mother said.

no mama, she is not a prostitute,My daughter remembers that "good name is better than silver and gold" and God's time is the best so said the Holy Bible, this Lagos you are going, is it not the Lagos that your classmate Mary went and came back with pregnancy? Instead of you to go there and bring shame for me, I prefer you remain here with me till God bring better Man for you.

Adanma said, Maama I am not a little girl, I know what I want from life, God is with me, nothing evil will happen to me, the mother replied "I don't know why you children of this days don't listen to parentaladvice, anyway don't forget praying toGod and avoid bad friends because I heard that every rich man in Lagos doesrituals and fraud business" Adanma replied, "Ah Maaama what about Doctors, Lawyers, Engineers and Pastors in Lagos?", not all the rich people are bad people, besides I am not going to Lagos in searchofmen, but to look for job that will enable me further my education.

Adanma said to her mother, worry not about me, just keep praying for me because I have grown up to understand that life itself is full of risk, don't you know that those who are afraid of life and those who refused to take risk, will end up been poor, Mama, no wonder you and papa are poor because you too were afraid to go to city and to take risk.

Shut up your mouth, don't you know that your father did not have anybody in the city; yes I know that papa never had any helper, but why didn't grandpa I mean your father and her children helped papa to the city?That is why I want to break that yoke fromour family.

 Already it was getting dark atnight,looking at the thick darkness it was like 1am midmorning, her friend was expecting her to come by 6am,Adanma could not sleep she was awake although the night waiting for daybreak, her mother continued talking as she also was half asleep and half awake and she said to Adanma, I was told in the meeting that all the girls in the city are doing no good job than prostitution, Adanma said that is not true, many girls in the city are working with big companies , some are doing marketing and the same time schooling like my friend she is working and schooling, and that's what I intend doing when I get to Lagos.

By the time, it was getting late about 2am,Adanma was half asleep and half awake, she was awake watching the time never wanting to miss the time, but to her it seems like the night was longer than the day, at a time she dosed off and had a dream of a new life in Lagos were everything was moving on well with her, she woke up happy and began to say "I claim it,and I will make it in Lagos in Jesus name, her enthusiasm increased she was very excited about the dream, she looked at the clock it was 5. Am, she jumped up say her prayers ,woke up her mother, and went straight to brush her teeth,take her bath and picked her bags set to leave.

 Meanwhile the village vigilante groups were at watch, no one walks out or comes into the village until the church mission early morning bell rings. She was watching the time anxiously waiting to hear the church mission bell, which was the only way the people of the village could know that the day is dawn and free for everybody to move about for works and business.

 Just few munites to 6am, the mission bell ranged, it was 6 am, she hurriedly carried her bags both her mother and few young relatives were waiting for her, having their lamps on to escorther to the next village where her friend was already standing outside beside a taxi she hired that will convey them to the town at the Lagos transport terminal.

The whole village was still very dark because there was no electricity and there were many big trees along each sides of the road, her friend was already worried and agitated about the delay, because her program was to catch the first bus to Lagos "Does this village girl think that journey to Lagos is a simple one?She ranted, as she was talking gazing at the road, she saw two lights like a Lamp coming fromafar; she said "this must be her coming no other person could move by this time since today was not the big market day.

 And just as she was talking,Adanma finally arrived with her old mother and family members who escorted her to bid her farewell. Adanma said to her friend, "Ngozi, good morning and her friend responded with little cold mood of annoyance indicated in her voice that she was not happy with her, she said "I've been standing outside here with this taxi driver waiting for you since 5am, don't you know that journey to Lagos is a very long journey? Did you not remember that I told you to wake up early?

Adanma replied "Ngooo, I am very sorry", you will not believe that I was awake since 1am ready to come out" Ngoziburst out laughing and said 'why' were you awake by that time, didn't you sleep yet you came out late? Adanma said "Ngooo, I didn't want to miss the journey but one cannot cheat nature, I didn't know how I suddenly felt asleep "My sister please don't be angry with me I am very sorry.

 This is my mother 'Ngozi greeted her Mama Good morning; Adanma Mama responded "Good Morning my daughter,don't be angry with your friend, please my daughterI beg you ,trully we came late, she raised the Lantern up to her face trying to see her face, she asked, my daughter how are you? Whose daughter are you? Do I know your parents?My daughter told me you are the one she is following to Lagos; I am very surprise also very happy that God sent you to help my daughter out from this village.

Mama, I am the daughter of MaziOkeke the meat seller, Adanmas mother exclaimed "Okeke that sells meat at the OrieAma Market? My own Okeke? Yes he is my father but late, It happens that Adanma's mother and MaziOkeke wife came from one kindred meaning that Ngozi and Adanma has an extended maternal relationship through their maternal home.

 The old woman was very happy and relaxed, her fears were gone,she began to bless them and the taxi driver was busy arranging their bags in the boot after that, the driver drove off,Adanma was waving hands to her mother saying, Mama bye, bye, her crying mother was waving at her also together with her relations as the car drove off from the village, they stood waving at the taxi till it goes faraway from their sight.

CHAPTER 27

It was a very long journy indeed coming to Lagos, Adanma counted how many houers it took the driver to get to lagos at night and he counted how many states they passed.

When they got to the border of Lagos , she saw the inscription written boadly on a sign post, THIS IS LAGOS. From that morment she became very ensited and was looking at the beautiful buildings , cars and too many crowd of people moving about.

That night they got to Ngozi apartment so late and very tired, it was a very little one room apartment she lives, she has no bed just a little 6/6 foam she kept on the capetted floor with her standing fan, 6 inchs television and her cooking stove , pots and plates.

The compound was like a barracks with many tenants and general toilet, in the morning some neighbors came to welcome Ngozi from home and they saw Adanma ,

Ngozi introduced Adanma to her neighbors saying, this is my sister and my childhood friend, her name is Adanma , they all well comed her as they shook hands with Adanma.

Few days latter, Ngozi told her friend to wise up because this is Lagos, she added that here in lagos most girls and ladies suvives through men and a beautiful girl as you, will not find it dificult to suvive here in Lagos but you must be wise, Adanma asked how? Do you mean that ladies give out their bodies to men for suvival? Yes we do Ngozi replied, God forbid me do that, Adanma said.

Adanma please tell me , what how do you think you can suvive in Lagos without playing out with men? There is no job any where in this city, Ngozisaid.Adanma replied, but you told me that you are do marketing job in Lagos?, yes that is the job I do Ngozi said, for which company are you working? Please take me along maybe I might be employed too, Adanma said.

Ngozi smiled and said, I am self employed I don't work for anybody, if you want to join me, therefore get raedy to follow me out this night to Apapa, that is where we do marketing with other beautful ladies.

Adanma was astonished at what she was hearing and she ask, what product is that which you market at night? Ngozi replied, do you mean you don't understand all I am trying to explain to you since? It is a prostitution job, we market our selves to men at the club, that is my work, you are free to join me.

Adanma said, God forbit me do that, I rather go back to village than to do such work, Ngozi became angry with her and she said, if you don't join me, be ready to provide for your self all basic things including feeding because, this is Lagos., every body you see here fends for them selves, I can notcary your borden.

From that morment, Adanma began to think of way out as she refused to join her friend in prostitution. One day she tried going out to the nearby streets in search of job, having known no body, lockly she find her first job at a resturant as a sales girl.

The job was very tidious and very charlenging for her, every man that comes there to drink,all would ask her out, butinteligently she will refuse their offers politely, and always very chearful to every customers .

 One day the owner of the restaurant who was watching every thing about her closely, confirmed that Adanma was avery good and hard working, always sincere andaccurate in her account recording of every sells she made, her presence boosted the business more than ever, as many customers were trooping in with their friends and family members day by day to have a drink and to eat good food,thisatitude made her madam to trust and loved her so dearly, that she began to show her love in return.

CHAPTER 28

One day Adanma made up her mind to accept any man that showed her love, such a man shall be my lover and he must be a single young man that is educated and a working class person, a man that loves God that will take good care of her, she said.

Adanma has never falling in love with any man neither has she slept with any man before at her age of 21 years.

At the restaurant, defferent men comes there to drink and eat, many of the men loved her maner of services and approach to customers, more expecialy one MrSegunAdemola, a banker who often come to the restaurant at the close of his work, he so much loved Adanma, that he could hardly sleep at night without thinking of her beauty and her good manners.

One day, he summoned courage to engaged her on a relationship talk, to his amazement, Adanma gave him audience and accepted his proposals, the man was very happy that night and began to take care of Adanma like a God sent man to her.

Every week he buys her new beautiful dresses and shoes, wrist watches and many other good things.

Adanma was interested to learn Yoruba language from him and Segun was also interested to learn Igbo language from her and they both began to teach each other the simple communication words, each time they are to gether, such as:

YORUBA   ENGLISH..   IGBO

WA..............................COME......................BIA

MALO .... GO.............................GAWA

JOKOO............................ SIT DOWN..................NODI ODO

IJOKOO............................ CHIAR......................OCHE

ONJEE.............................. FOOD.....................ERI MERI

OMI .... WATER........................NMIRI

INO..
LIGHT..........................OKU

IGBALE...............................
BROOM...AZIZA

ASHO..CLOTH......................................
AKWA

OMO...CHILD... NWA

IYAWO.......................................WIFE....................................... NWINYEN

OKO...HUSBAND................................... ....DI

So they laughed and had a very good time that day, learning each other language, yet Adanma refused every request he made on her,she said until she get married, and such is not her priority at the morment, I have an ambition to school further she said.

Shegun was interested at zeal, he asked, if you have the opportunity to further your education, what course would like to study and dream do you have?

Adanma smiled and said she wants to study medicine as to become a medical doctor in future, that's my life dream and goal she said.

Segun replied, that's a very good dream and good course you have chosen, but you need to pass your entire sience subject with biology, chemistry, physics, mathmatis and other.

Adanma responded that she had the highest grade in her siencesubjets, Shegun was very happy with her and he promised to link her up with the T .Y. DANJUMA FOUNDATION, an organization that stands out to help the poor people more expecialy girl child education and empowerment is their utmost priority.

That was how Adanma through these foundation, she was able to school further and achieved her dream and she was married to mrShegun who stood by her till she became that which God had destined her to be.

I WILL LOVE TO HEAR FROM YOU

For any enquirery or do want us to visit your organization to speak to the pulpils,

Please call +234 8176991430.

Email.Chidiricard77@gmail.com, richardschidi420@gmail.com

ABOUT THE BOOK

ADANNMA THE HEROIC GIRL, is a story formulated to re tell the success story of most Nigeria women through these this literature book as to encourage the younger generation woman.

 An African woman is a virtures woman with great potential that is capable to manage, inprove and provid care for her family, even to lead a Nation, women like Queen Amina of Zaria. FunmilayoRansomeKuti. Queen Moremi of Yoruba land, Florence NwanzuruahuNkiruNwanpa of Igbo land, Nana Asmau, the daughter of UsmandanFodio of Sokoto, Margaret Ekpo of CrossRiver state, Chief Elizabeth AbimbolaAwoliyi and many more.

Adanma the heroic girl literature book, explains the true spirit of African woman that can survive anywhere, even with just a little given resourcess or chance, she could change her evironment positively, she is that woman which the great king Solomn, discribed in the bible . Pro, 31 v 10 -31.As virtures woman.

But very painfuly and unfortunately for the African women, the African political, tradinal and religional system and structurs, does not give them the chance to contribute their leadership potencials, rather they are put behind the men in all the sectors .

The book is about a little girl whose parents were not intersted to her educational dream ,simplly because she is a girl child.

Several years ago, in the acient time, girl child education was not concidered very important by most parents and communities in Africa.

Therefore, Adanma was eiger to go to school, because she has a dream to become a successful woman in her life, but the system never gave her the oportunity yet she didn't give up, till she could made it.

 The book is written with clear narraives and with a very simple and understandable grammar for class an,d it a age, also it contains a summarise portions of moral slesions from each chapter of the book, with selected bible back up verses, that will spiritually broading the knowledge of our children

Her story line, represents the success story of many Nigeria successful women whose names were mentioned in this book, many of them were never born with silver nor golden spoons, yet they could make it to the top because of their choice and self discipline policy.

The entire contents of the book, are in segments of different highlights of events, such include:

(A) The Igbo traditions on agriculture.

 (B) The Igbo tradition on marriage .

(C) The challenge of girl child education in the ancient age.

(D) The truth about new yam festival and the blessings.

(E) Student lives and the danger of peer group pressure.

(F) The price and rewards of determination.

Adanma the heroic girl, is a book for every child, it shows how determination and diligence rewarded a little girl who grew up wisely, focusing all her time and mind to achieve success in her life, simply because she discovered that she came from a very humble background, which would have been a very good excuses and reasonr for any other girl in her condition to be come a waward girl .

 But yet, she refused to surrender her ambition to her misfortunes, rather she developed a very strong will, which became her strength and the driving force that saw her although.

This book contains lots of moral lessons which every girl child will learn from, it contains some basic Igbo cultures, needed to be passed unto the younger generation that will certainly educate their minds also entertain the reader.

Rev Dr. Richards Ernest Chidi

www.ingramcontent.com/pod-product-compliance
Lightning Source LLC
Chambersburg PA
CBHW071620150726
48000CB00004B/1811